D0777658

UNTANGLED

A STORY OF RESILIENCE, COURAGE, AND TRIUMPH

ALEXIS ROSE

Note to Reader:
This story is the recollection of my life. All names and locations have been changed. Some descriptions of the events were changed for flow of the narrative and to protect the innocent and the not so innocent.

Untangled includes descriptions of sexual and physical abuse. Some readers may find some of these written accounts triggering. If this happens, the reader is advised to stop reading and consult a mental health professional.

Edited by Suzanne Fry
Cover Design: K. Leopold
Front Cover Photographer: Janet Rosauer
Front Cover Model: Naomi Peiffer

Available from Amazon.com, Kindle and other retail outlets

www.atribeuntangled.com
atribeuntangled@yahoo.com

ISBN-13: 978-1514213223
ISBN-10: 1514213222

Miss Suzy by Miriam Young, ©1964 by Parents' Magazine Press

For all the survivors I met along the way.

Contents

Foreword

On a cool Colorado morning in June, I guided Alexis and her daughter up the switchbacks leading to the summit of a 14,000 foot peak. With the tree line below us, I watched the two extraordinary women in front of me scramble up the rocks and obstacles that stood in their way. The air was thin, especially for us flatlanders, requiring frequent rests and breaks. Near the apex, we sat and reflected upon the remarkable journey that Alexis had been on. On that day, she showed the same courage and tenacity that she had shown through our years of therapy together. She made it evident that nothing would deter her from summiting. It was the literal realization of the metaphorical journey that we had been on.

Climbing a mountain. This was the early metaphor that we adopted to describe the healing process. My role was that of Sherpa; I was there to guide the way, keep her safe, and help carry some of her burden. Her job was to keep putting one foot in front of the other, to trust the process, and to honor my requests for her to slow down and rest along the way.

Over the course of our time together, Alexis has taught me a great deal about the human capacity for growth and change. That tenacity helped mediate the incredible sadness, sorrow, and horror that came with my bearing witness to the abuse and torture she endured during the first half of her life.

As serendipity would have it, we share some common beliefs. We have a mutual respect for one another, a shared love for all the ways the F-word can be used in the English language, similar humor and spiritual beliefs. All of these things have been a gift as we worked to untangle the extraordinary mess that trauma left behind.

I am indebted to her in so many ways. She has been a steadfast example of the parent I aspire to be. She has broadened my awareness of world politics and the unfortunate path the intelligence community has at times followed. She is the embodiment of courage, and I have stolen many of her mantras along the way. She has made me a better psychologist and a better human being, and for this I am eternally grateful.

~Kevin

Introduction

Six years ago my repressed past began erupting to the surface. My mind felt like a war zone. If I had painted a picture of it, the buildings would have been in rubble with broken rock everywhere, blocking the streets as if a bomb had gone off. Everything is in ruins. Stray dogs and vacant, shell-shocked people silently wander what's left of the streets.

My body is streaked with sweat and dirt from my desperate search to find safe shelter. I'm barefoot, in a grimy torn t-shirt and shorts; my hands and feet caked with dirt. My hair is filthy and matted. My mouth is dry; I can smell and taste the gritty dust that hangs in the air. I sit down on a curb at the side of the road, and I know it's over.

I'm unbelievably weary, all my energy spent in the act of sitting down. I'm devastated…emotionally, mentally, and physically, and the worst of my wounds are invisible. My eyes fill up, but no tears fall. I can only sit amid the rubble, trying to trust the safety of the gray, silent sky.

Six years later, the scene has changed. I'm no longer living in fear of the tangled web of sadistic people who use threats to keep their victims terrified and questioning their sanity. I feel grateful. The therapist that I call my Sherpa is sitting next to me. He's listened to and witnessed my entire story, and never deserted me. He understands my journey and sometimes shares my grief. He's helped me honor my resilience; taught me the value of telling my story and the importance of just sitting with my truth. So we sit here together, quietly resting in that truth.

I've fully remembered and told the story of my first twenty years, of surviving the abuse, neglect, abandonment, and fear. I've left behind those who terrorized me. I've untangled myself. My courage has set me free, and now nothing can keep me tied to the past. I can truly live today with blinders off and eyes wide open.

PART 1

Chapter 1
WHATS A HOUSE GOT TO DO WITH IT?

Most of us remember the nuances of the houses we grew up in. We know the nooks and crannies, and the sounds the house makes when it settles and groans. We know the clicking noise of the furnace kicking in, the whistling sound of the wind blowing through the windows, and how the gate slams as someone makes their way to the door. We can trust our way in the dark during power outages or to sneak food from the refrigerator at midnight, because we know where the furniture is and where the stairs begin and end.

I lived in three different houses growing up, the first two in Michigan and the third in Minnesota. Each move brought more carpeting. I lost the early warning system that wooden floors and creaky steps gave me as the carpet grew wall-to-wall.

The first nine years of my life I lived in Grant. I remember everything about that house. I could draw it in great detail; actually I could draw all three houses in great detail. I liked this house the best, not only because the floors and stairs were wooden and creaky, but because I shared it with all my siblings at the same time. My parent's attention was divided between the four of us children. When I was nine and we moved to the suburbs, the attention shifted away from my siblings and the spotlight fell directly on me.

Inside that first house my bedroom was my refuge because of the windows. My sister and I had beds beneath the two windows looking out towards the front of the house. There was another window with a window-seat on the side of the room that faced the neighbor's house. During the day I would sit on the window-seat and read. Most nights as I lay in bed, I would turn my head towards that same window and imagine fire consuming the side of the neighbor's house; intense bright orange flames licking high into the air. I was young but I was already finding ways to externalize the pain that was coursing through my body.

The living room was large and filled with gray furniture covered in thick plastic that you stuck to in the summer and froze on in the winter. The dining room had a fireplace along one wall, double glass doors leading to a porch, and a swinging door leading into the kitchen. That swinging door would make an earsplitting banging sound when an angry parent would smack it open when coming into or going out of the dining room. The kitchen had ugly dark green linoleum and two steps leading from it that either led you outside, or if you turned right, led you down a steep set of stairs into the basement. The basement had a large room where the boys would use their wood burning sets and a corner where my father had his easel set up, a place where he would draw charcoal portraits of the family and neighbors.

Aside from the linoleum in the kitchen and the concrete of the basement the rest of the house had hardwood floors and stairs. A few area rugs covered the center of the rooms but they did nothing to mask the sound of people walking or climbing the stairs.

The backyard seemed huge to me as a little girl. We had a few apple trees, cattails growing behind the garage, and a round swimming pool. I remember the wild raspberries that grew against the chain link fence.

I played alone in that backyard for long periods of time. My refuge was behind the garage in a corner along the neighbor's fence. There I stayed hidden, out of sight from all the windows on the back of the house and the porch. Standing behind the garage, hearing my heart beat like a hummingbird, I petted the cattails that grew by the fence. I picked the tiny purple violets to make bouquets that I would grip as tightly if they were my last friends in the world. I didn't care that they wilted with the heat of my hands; I just wanted to look at the delicate petals and drink in their color. It was a solitary existence but solitary was far better than any kind of attention that I received inside of that house.

The energy inside our house was super-charged. Tension crackled in the air like electricity, no matter how many of us were inside. If there wasn't some kind of abuse going on, there was a silence that hung so thick and heavy that I would find myself looking down at the floor, or fidgeting, not knowing what to do with my hands. Opera or classical music sometimes blared from the stereo, a macabre contrast to the silence. At other times the volume of the music would alert us to what was going to happen next; the rising crescendo seemed to egg my parents on and steel us for explosive abuse.

Mealtime was dreadful for all of us except for my father. We were required to sit around the table in silence, with impeccable manners. My father would be served his favorite foods that he didn't share with anyone else. My mother loathed all things domestic, so mealtime was agony for her. Every meal came with a serving of bitter looks and sighs. You could cut the tension with a knife, and I often felt as if I wanted to explode into screams to release my anxiety. If one of us spilled our milk, the meal deteriorated into my mother shrieking and my father berating us on how stupid we were.

We didn't play together as kids. My two older siblings (ten and eight years older than I was) hated each other, and my brother who was two years older than me wasn't my playmate. The only sibling bonding moment I remember was when I was eight years old. My brother Adam and I were in my room sitting on the window seat. We were listening to my mother scream at my brother while my father beat him so horrifically that it sounded like two animals in a fight to the death. Adam and I stood up and hugged each other as tight as we could, saying over and over, "I wish they would all die, I wish they would all die." That experience didn't really bond us. We simply shared the childish belief that if we both wished our family dead, it had a better chance of coming true than one of us doing it alone.

I have vague memories of sitting on the basement stairs listening to Thomas' band rehearse, and glimpses of my sister playing guitar on her bed and singing sad folk songs. Once a year the four of us were forced to sit in the living room for a family photo. When I see these pictures now, I see Lucy and Adam looking vacant and detached, and Thomas aching to be loved.

Even though the four of us were living under the same roof, we had completely solitary existences. The only connection between my siblings and I was dark and abusive, passed down from the older to the younger ones. My sister was cruel to my older brother. She verbally abused him, calling him stupid. She used my father's love against him at every turn. My older brother was brutally violent to my brother Adam. I remember Thomas punching Adam in the stomach the day after Adam came home from having surgery.

I grew up hyper-vigilant, always on alert, knowing that anything could happen. I knew who was coming up the stairs by the sound of their footsteps. I just didn't know if they were coming for me or would pass me over for my brothers. The creaky floors warned me about who was walking and where they were headed.

We moved to our second house the summer I turned nine. My sister had gotten married and moved to Puerto Rico. My brother Thomas moved in with us for a few months and he and Adam shared a room while I had a room to myself. At first I loved having my own room with its beautiful blue carpeting. I wanted to believe that since we moved, things would be different. They *were* different but not in the way that I expected. Nothing got better. I had a hard time acclimating to the house in the suburbs. It was bland and ugly with fewer rooms and even fewer places to hide. I couldn't hear what was happening below me when I was in my room or, above me if I was in the basement. The house was too new.

Even though I didn't like this new house, there were definite positives about moving to the suburbs. There were kids my age in our neighborhood and I began to make friends. I suddenly had real playmates and I was able to go to their houses or roam around the neighborhood. I was freed from hiding behind the garage in the backyard of our first house. In our new complex there was a pool and a clubhouse with ping pong and pool tables, plus a room upstairs where kids would gather to watch *Soul-Train* after school. When I wasn't grounded for months at a time, I would hang out in the clubhouse with older boys and girls, who took me under their wing and gave me my first taste of whiskey. One of the guys was a man in his twenty's named Craig that I eventually sold drugs for in high school.

We lived in the Sheridan house for seven years, until my parents decided to move to Minnesota. They left me homeless for a few months, but I joined them on my 17th birthday. Moving into that small, quiet suburb felt like culture-shock for me. The new house had thick white carpeting and chandeliers everywhere, even the bathroom. It also housed an incredible negative energy, and I always felt fearful and unsafe there. I know now that the negative energy I was feeling belonged to the people who inhabited it, but at the time it was easier to blame the building.

After my father died and my mother moved to the Middle East, I only allowed myself to live in any one place for a few years. I kept moving because I felt that at any moment, I might be betrayed by the very structure that was meant to protect me. That rule, one of many I imposed on myself, spoke to how desperate my need for safety was, and to the level of fear that I had lived with.

Chapter 2
THE WOODS

I am a first generation American. Both my father and mother immigrated after World War II and brought with them, layer upon layer of secrets from their past. My mother emigrated from Germany to Boston; my father emigrated from Hungary by way of Calgary, to Boston. Both came from complicated upbringings and the horrors of war. My mother's strong European bloodline and my father's tragic life story helped me eventually understand, but not excuse, their willingness to betray their own daughter for the good of a country.

By the time I was five years old, I already had hopes and dreams of being able to live alone. I had a book called *Miss Suzy*, about a squirrel who lived alone high atop an oak tree. Miss Suzy cooked, cleaned, and sang all day. At night, she was lulled to sleep by the gentle wind and the stars. One day a band of red squirrels sneaked into her house, broke all her things, ate up all her food and chased her away. Homeless and rain-soaked, she climbed a tree and found another home in the attic of an old house. She lived in a doll house where she found a box of toy soldiers who came to life. When Miss Suzy told them about what happened to her in the oak tree, the soldiers marched up the tree, kicked out the red squirrels and Miss Suzy moved back home.

In my five year old mind, this tale had many relatable metaphors. I compared myself to the story's heroine. It gave me hope that I could also live alone in a tree, and I began dreaming up ways to escape my family. But I knew, even then, that unlike Miss Suzy I wasn't going to be rescued by a group of chivalrous soldiers. I knew that all the adults in my life were the same. They kept secrets and participated in secret ceremonies.

By the age of eight, I had already been exposed to a great deal of ritualistic abuse and it had taken its toll. Like most abuse victims I ached for someone to rescue me, but I also knew that I wasn't living in anything like a story book. My world was vastly different from that of other young girls. In my world children didn't get rescued, they were silenced with threats of death. They lived with the constant fear of being killed. I loved the *Miss Suzy* book because she was so happy living on her own, after the toy soldiers saved her home. She didn't need anyone else in her life, she was safe and happy.

By a very early age, I had stopped hoping that my family would be vanquished by a company of toy soldiers. I knew the only way out of my situation was if I left and found my own place to live. Instead of an oak tree, I began to fantasize about living beside a deep blue lake surrounded by soft sand and white cliffs. As I look back, that fantasy of taking control, leaving my family and finding a peaceful existence, nourished my amazing ability to survive.

When I look at pictures of myself when I was a youngster, it amazes me how tiny I was. I was the youngest of four and the only one looking into the camera with big brown eyes and dark hair. My siblings all had blond hair and blue eyes; I looked like my father and my siblings looked like my mother. I was so disconnected from myself that looking at photos was the only way I could convince myself that I was a real person; alive and part of a family.

At an early age, I began collecting odd things like rocks, a bag of dirt, a lock of hair, a cuff-link, or anything that I thought would provide proof of my existence. I hid these things in safe places all over my room. I didn't keep too many of them in one place for fear that someone would find my cache and I would lose my whole collection.

I thought these artifacts could prove where I was, what was happening to me, and who was with me. In my mind these were my smoking guns. I was already trying to gain control over my young life and circumstances. I couldn't have known that years later, these would be precious breadcrumbs for me to follow as I began recovering my repressed childhood memories.

I was living in a world of secrets. I was born into a family with a strong European bloodline. I was indoctrinated into the family rules at a very young age, at the hands of my grandparents, uncle, aunt, and father. The secrets involved inter-generational abuse, incest, and seasonal secret society rituals.

At a very early age I'd learned to disconnect from myself and either watch what was happening to me from afar, or try to project the pain outside of my body. When I was abused at night, I would find a window in the bedroom and imagine the house next door on fire. I saw the flames shooting up the sides of the house in vivid orange and red; the heat and the spiky flames consuming the house. I found a way to externalize and dissociate from the pain and humiliation.

That fire raged outside my window most nights until we moved to Sheridan the summer I was nine. That fire and my dream of living alone on the lake were my golden thread of survival. That thread kept the pieces of my shattered soul together, and gave me the strength I needed to wake up and face another day. My raging fires were imaginary, but there were countless times in my young years that I had witnessed real and frightening rituals. These took place in the fall and spring with a group of six men, five others and my father.

They took place in temple basements, houses, or the woods and once, even in a mausoleum. They were held in the fall and spring of each year around full moons or holidays. They seemed very elaborate in my young mind. The men were dressed in robes, with candles burning and someone holding a staff with an ornate gold medallion on the top. In shadows cast by the candles, they chanted, sometimes handled snakes, and engaged in ritualistic child abuse.

The fall rituals were held in the woods of Wallingford, Michigan. I may have been taken to the woods before the age of seven, but that year was a turning point for me. I began to understand how dire my situation was becoming. It was a sunny but cool autumn day with brightly colored leaves on the trees. I was sitting next to a teenage girl who told me her name was Jennifer. She looked beautiful to me, with long blond hair that would blow back from her face with the wind. She was wearing a plaid shirt and jeans. She looked to me like a free spirit who belonged at a folk concert singing and dancing, but instead, she was on edge. Just like me, she was a frightened child watching the men in the clearing.

Without warning, Jennifer got up and started running onto the trails to the left of us. My only thought was to run after her. She veered to the right and I stayed straight. From the sounds of leaves crunching behind me, I knew someone was closing in on me. Before I had time to think, one of the men caught up with me, grabbing me from behind.

He pulled me along the path to meet up with the others who had run after Jennifer. I saw the men standing in a semi circle. Jennifer was on the ground in front of them. She was laying quiet and still, her pretty blond hair covering her eyes. I don't know how long I stood there but I do remember one of the men saying to me, "This is what happens to girls who run away." As a man led me away from the clearing, I remember wishing that I could have pushed Jennifer's hair away from her face. I didn't want her pretty hair to be so messy in front of those men, and I wondered how could she see what was happening to her, with her hair over her eyes.

That thought and her image haunted me into my adulthood. I don't know for sure what happened to Jennifer that day. She may have just been knocked out or something more sinister may have befallen her. The men weren't done with their rituals for the day. They built a fire, carried in a tiny goat that made sounds like a baby, cut its throat and did more ceremony. I remember watching the men with the smoke rising and the smell of burning animal flesh and blood. I remember feeling terrified. Everything seemed to happen so fast that day. What horrified me was that Jennifer was lying in a clearing in the woods, and the men never stopped their perverse festivities.

A few days after the incident in the woods, I took the chance to stray from the safety of my backyard. I was sitting on my neighbor's front steps looking at a little mirror with a red plastic case. I looked up and saw my mother storming down the street yelling at me. I panicked when I saw her, dropped the mirror and ran; but not before I heard it shatter on the concrete. My mother shrieked at me as she followed me back to our house. She came in and stood in the kitchen with my father, and I lost it. I started screaming at them that I knew what happened in the woods and that they had killed Jennifer.

My parents became enraged. My mother started toward me and I instinctively turned to run down the two steps leading to the back door, not thinking about the basement steps to the right of me. I thought I felt a push and the gut-wrenching surprise of losing my balance and falling down the basement stairs. I grabbed the railing to stop myself, and felt my hip come down hard as I tugged in the other direction to stop my fall. I groped my way to the bottom of the stairs, hurt and stunned only to look up to see my parents standing on the steps.

My father looked down at me and said, "You are dead to us; and you will *never* talk about what happened the other day." I was in pain, confused and terrified but I knew they were serious. They had looks of utter disgust on their faces. I vowed to myself that I would never talk about what happened in the woods and I believed I was dead to them. After what I had witnessed in those woods, I had every reason to believe anything they said. I only was seven years old.

My parents ignored me between bouts of physical and sexual abuse, and started calling me by names other then my own. It was so confusing to me. I found a pair of eyeglasses on my desk in school one day and had no memory of having to wear glasses. They were just there after recess. I was getting so confused about my identity. Either I was dead to them and totally ignored, or being called other names like Bee, Dolphin, or Eleven. That is when the fantasy I had about living alone by the lake really began to take hold.

The next time I found myself back in the woods in Wallingford, I was sitting alone on a rise. This time there wasn't a fire burning on a sunny autumn day. It was cold, gray, and cloudy and from what I could tell I was the only kid at this gathering. I remember wearing a light blue windbreaker. I kept playing with the strings on the hood, pulling them up and down listening to them swish against the nylon jacket. Somewhere in my mind I had already partitioned off what had happened to Jennifer the year before.

I remember the leaves were turning colors and the woods seemed thicker and further away than in past years. The men were gathered around the open trunk of a car by the edge of the woods. Suddenly, I felt myself being jerked backwards and up. My hands instinctively clawed at my throat as I tried to get my footing and balance. My heart was pounding against my chest, and my mind was exploding with terror. One of the men had come up behind me and pulled me backwards with a rope around my neck. He jerked the rope but grabbed me with his arms too, to pull me up and into him. He told me to look over at the trees. When I glanced over, I saw something hanging and the men standing off to the side.

He led me to the trees and hanging there still and lifeless, was the little girl I knew as Sarah. She was one of the girls that I had sometimes seen at the rituals. I didn't think she had a home, but couldn't say for sure because we had never talked about anything. We had only held hands a couple of times when we were in the same room together. Sarah's head was drooping as she hung from the tree and her long black hair was hanging down towards her slack feet. One of the men grabbed my hand and made me touch her feet. They were bare and cold. He said, "This is what happens to girls who disobey the rules." Everything was surreal, the trees, the men, and the little girl I was touching. I was terrified but at the same time, I knew that Sarah would never suffer again.

I'm not sure how much time passed. It could have been minutes or hours, but eventually my father, who was one of the men standing there, told me it was time to go. I followed him to the car. As we were nearing the end of the grassy area I turned around to take one last look at Sarah. I was leaving her all alone but something inside of me, knew she was better off. She had escaped and wouldn't feel any more pain. As we drove home, my soul filled with dread, helplessness and abject loneliness.

When we got home I went upstairs, closed my bedroom door, walked to my dresser and drank what was left of my bottle of child-proof perfume. I didn't think about what I was doing. I was instinctively trying to end the pain of the day.

I was eight years old and I couldn't stand the pain of my existence any longer. One day after my mother screamed at me, I walked into my room, found a metal object and cut my left wrist.

I cut enough for it to bleed, not profusely, but enough for the blood to drip in a steady line.

I heard my mother tromping up the steps and opening my bedroom door to continue her tirade. She saw my wrist and was livid. She grabbed me by my arm and dragged me into the bathroom, threw me into the tub and began to hit me, screaming at me, "You stupid kid, how could you do this to me?" I blocked out most of what she was saying because I was mesmerized watching the blood drip in the white bathtub. Each time she hit me more blood smeared onto the tub. I didn't feel any pain and thought for a moment, that I had finally succeeded and found a way to end my suffering. But deep down inside, my chest and belly still hurt. I was filled with despair.

We moved during the following summer and I've never been back to the Wallingford woods. The world was topsy-turvy with national and international events taking center stage. The aftermath of the riots in Grant sent my parents to the suburbs and my father began traveling more and more.

The endless cycle of family, inter-generational, and ritual abuse continued until I was ten. That's when I was introduced to a whole new level of wretchedness.

Chapter 3
AGE TEN

My life took a dramatic turn when I was ten years old. I woke up one morning and I had entered womanhood. I had no idea what was happening when I found blood flowing out of me and a terrible cramping stomach ache.

In those days, we didn't learn about periods in school until the sixth grade, a year too late for me. My mother had never broached the subject of how my body would change as I matured; besides, she was the last person I could turn to in my state of panic. My sister was long gone and living in Puerto Rico, so I had no one I could ask about what was happening. Was I sick? Was I dying? Besides the panic, I was bewildered about what I should do next.

I did the only thing I could think of at the time. I took my bloody underwear and hid them in one of my drawers. I put layers of toilet paper in my clean underwear and went to school feeling anxious and sick. I spent the whole day wondering what was coming out of my body but was too embarrassed to go to the teacher or talk to a friend. After a long uncomfortable day all I wanted to do is go home, hide in my room, and figure out how to stop the bleeding.

When I got home from school that day I ran upstairs, opened my bedroom door and found my room completely torn apart. All my clothes were out of the closet, my drawers were emptied and upended, and everything on top of my dresser and shelves was in a heap and broken on the floor. Lying on top of the pile was the bloody underwear that I had hidden in a panic that morning; with a note that said, "You are Disgusting!" I felt horribly ashamed and embarrassed. As I crawled under the covers, I saw lying on the bedspread, a box that said maxi pads and a strange looking belt that I assumed went with the pads. I still had no idea what was wrong with me, but figured out how the pad fit on the belt, put it on and laid down, trying to figure out what I had done to myself the night before to wake up with blood dripping out of my body.

My mother never had any conversation with me about that day. She never explained that periods were normal or to expect them every month. She did continue to trash my room while I was at school with what I can only imagine must have been uncontainable rage towards me. She never destroyed my brother's room. Even though I was angry that I had to keep cleaning up my room and throwing away the things she broke, I felt some relief that she was taking her rage out on my belongings instead of my body or mind.

She must have told my father about my period, because he suddenly had no interest in me anymore. It was like I didn't exist. I no longer had to worry about making fire out the window at night. I knew that getting my period had a direct effect on how he treated me, but I didn't know why.

The other significant change when I was ten years old was that I took my first trip alone to somewhere other than to Boston where I had visited relatives. I don't really have any memory of being told that I was going out of town or being driven to the airport. My first vivid memory is of sitting on the airplane feeling nauseous and accepting the shiny silver airplane wings from the flight attendant. I remember the plane being smoky from cigarettes and the rough, bouncy ride. Even though the flight attendant gave me wings that matched hers to pin on my shirt, I recall still wanting to disappear and become invisible. That feeling of wanting to vanish was something I mastered at a very early age and I could feel it enveloping me on the plane.

When we landed a man and a woman were waiting for me at the gate. I didn't even think about it; I just went with them. I was actually relieved to find someone waiting for me since I had no idea why I had been put on the plane a few hours earlier. I walked out with them and got into a dark blue car. I remember the color of the car because my aunt drove a big dark blue sedan and even though this wasn't the same make and model, the color reminded me of being in Boston. Waves of nausea surfed through my system.

I had a habit of counting telephone poles whenever I was in a car. I figured that if I knew how many telephone poles I had passed I would be able to find my way home from wherever I was. I never thought to look at street names or landmarks, it was always telephone poles. After driving on the expressway for a while, we exited into the country. I had no more telephone poles to count. We were driving fast down a straight empty road with trees whizzing past me. All this was fueling my car sickness. My nausea turned to panic when we stopped in front of a low rise non-descript cement building. We were greeted at the door by a woman who was dressed the same way my drivers were dressed, in a dark blue suit. I hadn't really seen women dressed in suits before. I thought they all wore dresses, so it was kind of fascinating to see ladies wearing what I thought were men's clothes.

The woman brought me inside and took me to the elevators. She smiled at me and said, "Welcome. You are lucky to be one of the chosen ones." I didn't feel lucky, and I still didn't know where I was, or why I was there. I felt scared, sick, and very alone. When the elevator stopped, the woman took me to a room where there was a small cot with a pair of shorts and a t-shirt sitting on top of it.

She told me to change into the clothes lying on the cot and left the room. I stood there for a couple of seconds in a state of shock, wondering what I should do. Finally I got undressed and put on the dark blue shorts and the white t-shirt. I noticed as I was putting on my shirt that the sleeves were really cute and for a second, I felt really good in my new clothes.

That second of enjoying the clothes vanished immediately as the reality of my situation crept back in. I was sick with fear and anxiety as tears begin to well up in my eyes. When the woman opened the door again, I asked her if I could use the bathroom. She told me to leave my shoes and socks with the rest of my clothes and come with her. She led me to the bathroom and waited outside for me. I sat on the toilet looking at the bright white floor and let the tears fall down my face. After a few moments of crying I began to tell myself, "This can't be happening, this can't be happening," over and over again.

When I came out of the bathroom the woman in the suit asked me if I was okay, but didn't wait for an answer. She led me down the hall and into a room that was bright, cold and full of men in white coats. At least, that is what my ten-year-old mind took in at first glance. I was filled with dread, and when I turned around to get reassurance from the woman who had been my escort, she was gone.

From the time I walked through the doors of the building to when I was left alone in the room with the men in white lab coats was probably thirty minutes. Earlier that day I was a ten-year-old 5th grader who woke up, was driven to the airport and put on an airplane. By early afternoon I was standing in a facility somewhere in the countryside of another state, barefoot and terrified. I didn't feel lucky that I was chosen. I felt stomach-sinking dread.

Chapter 4
THE FACILITY

My earliest memory of being in the building tucked inside the trees was that there was a flurry of activity. I was weighed, measured, poked and examined, and asked a lot of questions. I was put through endless tests: matching, problem solving, fine motor skills and balance. No one explained what they were testing me for and I was too scared to ask. They fed me and instructed me not to flush when I used the bathroom. The testing went on for the first several hours of my stay, but then I was led to the room where I had gotten changed and told to rest. I sat on the cot and waited.

After a while, a woman appeared and told me to follow her. She took me to a room that was small and rather chilly. Waiting to greet me was a man in a white lab coat. There was a weird window that looked like a mirror that I now surmise was two-way glass. The man told me to sit down. He said he was going to show me a series of pictures and I was to tell him how the people in the photos were feeling.

At first, it was easy. The faces were of men, women and children with basic expressions of happy, mad and sad. I felt myself relax a little bit, although I was feeling cold as if the room was icing up. All I had on was shorts and a t-shirt. The man said that he noticed that I seemed cold and asked me if that was true. When I said yes he told me that if I got the next few feelings correct I could have a sweater. He showed me a few more pictures and I got them correct. The man was good to his word and gave me a sweater. Gratefully, it was too big for me and covered my legs. That helped me relax a little. He asked if I was ready to keep going and he reminded me that I had on a nice warm sweater because I had gotten the answers right by identifying how people were feeling.

When the next group of pictures came up I had some trouble naming the expressions on their faces. I didn't have the vocabulary at ten years old to identify someone looking anxious, worried, troubled or euphoric. Mixed into this next grouping were also some frightening images of insects and bloody car accidents. I believe I answered that entire grouping of photos wrong. At least the man thought I had. He told me to give back the sweater, and told me that if I wanted to wear it again I needed to focus on the feelings and identify them correctly.

The next group of images was similar to the first and I relaxed a bit again. I seemed to be getting them correct, but some of them were becoming disturbing. Every now and then there was a picture of a snake looking as if it was able to strike from the screen and bite. Each time I saw the picture of the snake I jumped and looked away. The man stopped the slideshow and told me to keep looking at the screen. He told me that even though I identified the feelings correctly, because I was acting out by moving around and being scared I couldn't have the sweater back. He changed the rules on me. I thought if I got the answers right I got the sweater, but now that wasn't true anymore.

I was getting weary from hours of testing. The room seemed to be getting colder and my hands and feet felt stiff. When the terrifying snake came up one last time and I put my hands protectively over my stomach, the man leaned in and told me, "The snakes will stay asleep if you remember that *surely* you cannot speak of anything that we help you learn here." He nodded towards the corner and someone came in to lead me out of that ice box of a room.

A woman walked me down a few corridors to the cage-like room with the cot and my clothes. She motioned for me to go inside, so I did. I'd had nothing to eat or drink since lunch and I was really hungry. As she was closing the door, she switched off the light. It was pitch black and silent. I crawled to the back corner with a blanket and got as small as I could. My mind was exhausted and I was starting to feel foggy and disconnected from myself. No one heard my screams that night as I woke up from a nightmare, or maybe they did.

The next day I was told to change into my own clothes and leave my shorts and t-shirt on the little cot. I was able to go to the bathroom to wash my face, brush my teeth and comb my hair before I was escorted to a little room and fed some breakfast.

A man who I would eventually think of as one of the "sirs" sat down across from me. He asked me my name. I told him "Alexis Rose." He said, "No, from now on we are going to call you Fearless Butterfly." He asked me if I liked butterflies. Of course I answered "Yes". In fact, I think I may have felt a little happy about being a butterfly. It seemed better to be a butterfly than a scared little girl. He said that I would be coming back some day but I was not to tell anyone what happened here, and that I was chosen to help "this great country of ours."

He asked, "Do you remember what happens if you tell secrets? Do you remember what happened in the woods to the two girls?" I didn't know how he knew those things but I nodded. He said, "Okay, very good," and left. I was brought outside and into the waiting blue sedan, and driven back to the airport. I was walked to the gate, and boarded a plane back home. I had a lot of time on that plane to try and forget everything that happened to me the day before. After all, I kept telling myself I had survived, and none of it mattered anyway. It was just one more day that I had to forget.

My mother was waiting for me at the gate when I got off the plane. She didn't say a word to me; she looked put out and seemed upset that she had to pick me up. We drove home in silence. I wondered why she wouldn't talk to me, but that was often the case. Sometimes, after my parents did something horrific to me, they would ignore me for days. I thought it was because they were mad at me for making them hurt me.

I couldn't wait to get back home. I almost ran into the house and up to my room. I found it bare of everything except my books and two stuffed animals. My dolls, toys, games and records were all gone. I went downstairs and asked where my things were, and my mother looked as if I had slapped her. She said that she had given them away to my teacher. His kids were here from Australia and had no toys of their own. I was so angry. My teacher had been at the school all year long and his kids probably had lots of toys. In fact I knew that he was close with a lot of families in my classroom, and that my mother was lying to me.

I spent the rest of the school year quiet and withdrawn. My nightmares increased after that first visit to the facility. I would hear a resounding, "Would you shut up?" coming from my parents' room when I woke up screaming. I was tortured by dreams of faces scrolling on a screen and of snakes striking, of big cold rooms with fluorescent lights and "sirs" invisibly watching me from behind windows. My young mind was being horribly damaged, and my identity stolen.

I went back to the facility a total of three times with my last visit when I was 11 years old. I had become almost robotic with the routine. I was prepared for everything and nothing. I had spent the last year of my life isolated and in fear, retreating further and further into solitude as my rattled and confused mind struggled from one day to the next.

I had grown accustomed to the florescent lights, the hallways and tunnels, the smells, pain and fear, the violence and odd requests that were made of my mind. I didn't have any fight left in me. I had lost any instinct to flee and often sat frozen in my tracks until they moved me to the next task. The last day I was there, they told me that I was ready for the next step, and that I would be called upon to use my newly acquired skills someday. I had no idea what they were talking about, because in my mind I had no new skills. I had nothing but pain and confusion.

They told me that the kids who had passed to the next level were going to have a special outing that evening. I suppose they were trying to make the last night special, but I had a sense that what was special to them would not be special to me.

I had long ago given up any hope of being happy, cared about, loved, or deserving of something special. I simply moved through my days like a little robot. At home I was shy and withdrawn. I still played with a few friends in the neighborhood but often found myself walking alone and aimlessly, living in a constant fog.

On that last day, we had gone over the skills of reading people's faces and emotions. I listened to recordings of languages and identified the accents. By this time I had become skilled at both. I no longer flinched at the snakes on the screen or felt the chill in the room.

After dinner I was escorted through the endless hallways and put in a room. It was different than the other rooms I had been in. This one had furniture that looked comfortable and had a real bed. The person who took me to the room left and I stood in the middle of the floor, just stood there like a statue. I wasn't interested in sitting or lying down on the bed. I simply stood there waiting.

Men I hadn't seen before began to make their way into the room. I'm not sure how many eventually came, at least three, maybe four. They were loud and jovial. It seemed as if I wasn't the only one who was receiving these visitors, because I heard something like, "Let's see what *this* little butterfly has to offer." I could feel my heart pounding in my chest and ears as these strangers violated my body, satisfying their individual perversions.

I don't remember anything after that. I'm sure my survival instinct took over and I dissociated.

My next real memory takes place the next morning. The same man that talked to me the first time I was taken to the facility was sitting across from me once again. He said, "You will not be coming back here again, and you will forget what has taken place while you were here unless you are called to use your skills." He continued, "Never speak of this place to anyone. If you do, you will *surely* die." And that was it; he got up, walked away and I never saw him again.

The time I spent at the facility had damaged my mind in a different way than the abuse or neglect I had suffered before age ten. My mind had been severely damaged by that training in the facility. Their reasons for doing this to me were beyond my comprehension then and now, but this wouldn't be the last time in my life that I would be used for some unknowable reason.

Chapter 5
LOOKING FOR MY IDENTITY

When I started junior high school my world opened up and I began to make new friends. I was quiet and withdrawn in my classes, and because there were so many other students I found it easy to make myself invisible. I never participated in class discussions or asked for help. My grades were good enough to keep things peaceful at home when report cards came, but not so good that I stood out to my teachers as a straight A student. Even though I was quiet and reserved with my new friends, I was still invited to parties on the weekends where there was a lot of booze and drugs.

I loved getting high. I found that it quieted my mind and made it easier to compartmentalize my life. I could actually feel happy at times. I had been dissociating from a very young age, but now I found I could literally forget where I lived and what my life was about when I left home each day.

I had learned to turn my life off when I left my house. I had no family, no home, no pain, and no abuse. My home life went black when I walked out the door. I felt no fear of inadvertently telling anyone what was going on with me for two reasons. One, I had been threatened so deeply that I knew not to trust any adults and two, I dissociated every time I left home.

I had honed the skill of forgetting the realities of my home life and the horrors that went with it so well, that sometimes when I got home, I was surprised at how unfamiliar my surroundings were when I walked through the door. Then, within seconds, the truth of my existence rushed back in. I knew where I was and who lived there.

I had also developed a false sense of security. I hadn't been back to the facility in months and no one seemed interested in me at home. It was silent there and I felt contentedly invisible. That was until one afternoon after school when my mother came upstairs and told me to get in the car. I didn't ask where we were going because something inside of me knew better. We drove to a beautiful old building in a neighboring suburb.

She dropped me off in the circular driveway and I was greeted by a man. I surmised what was in store for me. It had been about six months since I'd endured what happened that last night at the facility, but as soon as I saw that man it seemed like I had been there only yesterday. My stomach tied into a knot, I could hear my heartbeat in my ears.

I followed him into a room in the old building. There were several men on couches and chairs. The man who led me into the room turned and left me standing there, waiting. My eyes were locked on the floor as I felt someone approach and lead me by the arm to the center of the room. He began to undress me. The same sexual perversions that I had lived through on the last night at the facility were happening again.

I was humiliated, overcome with intense shame and fear. My brain was shutting down because I couldn't process the absurdity of all this. Just a few hours earlier I was having a normal day at school and now I was in the grip of the intense terror and shock of what was being done to me. I felt myself shut down emotionally and begin trying to compartmentalize what was happening.

When they were finished, someone tossed me my clothes. After I was dressed the man who escorted me from my mother's car took me back to her. She was waiting for me by the curb as if she was picking me up from school or a ballet class. I got in the car and slammed the door. She began to yell at me for making her wait so long because she had so much to do. She screeched,

"Why do you do this to me all the time?" The only emotion I could feel at that point was hate. I hated her.

This scenario where I was dropped off to become prey for the pleasures of men, played out a few more times in different locations and states before my 17th birthday. The places that I was being dropped off at became larger and more sophisticated. The parties were bigger and sometimes there were other children in adjoining bedrooms.

The scene was typically the same, I was escorted in, taken to a bedroom and would wait for one or two men at a time to come. Sometimes they would be drunk and laughing, sometimes I wondered if I was being filmed. It was disgusting and I was awash in shame each time someone new came in to take their turn. I felt that as each man got up to leave, they took another piece of my soul with them as they closed the door. That's the only way to describe how it felt. I turned off all my senses but deep inside, I felt as if my soul was in pieces, turning blacker, denser, smaller, and more tattered.

I became even quieter and more elusive with friends. I sought out drugs and I got comfortable with the escapism that mescaline and acid provided. I would smoke weed to take the edge off any feelings that would creep in around the edges. Whenever I could, I spent the night at someone's house so I wouldn't have to go home. My father was traveling more often and my mother ignored me completely unless she needed to present me for something. My brothers were strangers to me and my sister was a distant and occasional voice on the phone.

I would often wander around the neighborhood to stay out of the house. I met an older guy who lived nearby. Craig was twenty-six and a hard core drug dealer. He took me under his wing and let me stay at his house when he had parties.

I felt safe with him. He never touched me and the people at his parties ignored me. Craig was the first person to nickname me

"Mouse." He said I was as tiny and quiet as a sweet little mouse. It was a name that stuck throughout my teens. To this day, the people who know me from those years address my Christmas cards or emails to "Mouse." I used to empty Craig's ashtrays, help him pack up and distribute his drugs and sell his drugs, from my locker at school. I would do anything for him.

One day a friend of mine asked me who I got my drugs from and I mistakenly told him. I never thought he would seek Craig out on his own, but he did. Like everyone else he knew where Craig lived and went to his house asking to make a buy. Craig was furious that a young kid would come knocking on his door. I learned very quickly that I had made a big mistake telling Ron about Craig. The next time I saw Craig, he pulled over in his car, saying, "Hey Mouse, come here." He pulled out a gun and said, "Don't ever tell anyone who I am again. Do you understand?" "Yes," I stammered, "I understand."

I got that I had made a huge mistake. I also understood how precarious my one-sided friendship was with him was when he threatened me with his gun. I never went to his house again. I realized that even though I had felt a sense of safety with Craig, he was just as dangerous to me as the people in my life that I was trying to keep secret.

I grew more adept at keeping what was happening at home separate from my friends. They were living typical teenage lives. As the years went on and we moved to high school, my friends started dating. I had no interest in having a boyfriend. I couldn't conceive of having a normal life like my friends did. The times they would go off with boys or go to parties I would drift towards home.

When I was home, I found solace in my room with my records. It didn't matter how many times I had to put my room back together after my crazed mother tore it apart. Once I had my record player and records back on the shelf I was happy. If I sang the lyrics to the songs, I couldn't think about anything. Songs were safe, they couldn't hurt me. If a sad song caused some feeling of angst to pop-up, I could turn the music off and sit in the silence. Silence in my room, silence from my feelings, silence from my life.

Excerpt from my journal ~

The silence is the worst sometimes. Along with the moment when an abusive event ends the silence is sometimes the most uncomfortable part of being hurt. It's a strange feeling to see someone who has just hurt you in ways that are abhorrent turn around and walk away.

It feels as if they take a little piece of my spirit with them, leaving another tatter. It's not very often that my abusers say anything when they are finished. I think that's what makes the feeling of invisibility more palpable. No yelling, crying, blaming, scolding; they just simply finish and leave. It's a rather powerless feeling because they're not acknowledging me or what they did. I feel powerless, as if they were shredding my spirit, leaving me with a dark heaviness.

I may have been crying when they left. I know I was certainly in enough pain physically, sexually and psychologically to cry. Often times though, I would just stare at them as they left. Watching them go, I sometimes asked myself, why did that happen to me? But other times, I silently watched as they moved away from me, as if I didn't exist, as if what just happened didn't really happen at all. If they saw me on the street in five minutes, they wouldn't even remember who I was.

I can't remember a time when there wasn't silence in our house. There was terrible crescendo yelling, hitting, or other abuse, which often was accompanied by loud classical or opera music in the background, or there was a thick silence.

When my parents weren't abusing us, they were abusing each other; always followed by the silence. It is really hard to get your needs met when you are met with silence. Not just silence but also acting as if you are invisible. Dinner would still be prepared, but we would eat in silence. Rides would still be given, but given in silence. I would come home to my room turned upside down, which I imagined had been done in a screaming frenzy of rage, but by the time I got home, my destroyed room had a heavy echo of silence. My friends noticed it and there was nothing I could say; except my parents are mad at me.

Then the silence would be broken. It would be as if nothing had ever happened, except the yelling, screeching and name calling would begin again; an unnerving predictable pattern.

I felt invisible when I was being hurt and I felt invisible by the silence. I felt cold and lonely in the silence. It was as if nothing I said mattered enough for any response. Even if I did something wrong, like take the car without permission or come home late, or come in smelling like I smoked a pack of cigarettes and a bag of weed, there was nothing. To me it felt like another layer of abuse. Silence was used by my parents, the people in the facility, the people overseas and by my siblings.

Silence was a powerful weapon in their arsenal. Even after the threats stopped there was a weird silence. There was no reason to keep threatening me, I'm used to the silence that accompanies the "after of an event." Even now, I know that if I scream from the highest mountain top and accuse my perpetrators, it will only be met with silence; a punishing silence.

I meditate to bring a peaceful silence to my mind and spirit. I know the difference between a peaceful silence and a punishing silence. For mere moments, I'm not invisible when I meditate, I'm connected and I matter as part of the universe and then it fades and I feel the pain-silence.

Chapter 6
THE SPRING OF '74

Moon Mantra~
There is a full moon outside my window. It's just a moon.
Always waxing and waning. Just a moon and it is
beautiful.

I associate spring and fall full moons with ritualistic
ceremonies. Twice a year a group of six men, including my father
met to act out their secret society rituals. In the fall we gathered
in the woods; in the spring it was at the temple. The last time I
was tangled in one of these rituals was the spring of 1974 when I
was fourteen years old. I drew two conclusions from that event
that I carried into adulthood. The first was that the full moon was
no longer an innocent bright orb in the night sky. The second
was that I knew that God hated me.

That day in May of '74 we pulled into the parking lot of the
temple in downtown Grant. We parked by the nondescript side
door that we always used for these rituals. The front doors were
big, old, wooden ones that felt welcoming when we went inside
to pray.

I hadn't been to this temple since I was eight or nine years
old. That was when men in purple robes put snakes on my
stomach and showed me small dead animals, while candles cast
scary shadows on the stone walls. As they chanted, they taught
me a rhyme about how to kill myself if I ever forgot the rules
about keeping silent.

That spring day as we descended the basement stairs, I felt my stomach begin to clench in terror. I smelled the wax before I saw the candles. When I saw the men in their hooded robes, my brain froze. I ran to the corner of the room, crouched down, and started to crawl as far as I could into the wall. I pushed against it thinking I could escape into it. I knew that something awful was about to happen, and I could feel the hair on the back of my neck standing up.

As I tried hard to burrow inside of the wall, someone came up behind me and yanked hard on my hair. This sent me scrambling backwards. He put his arms around my body, lifted me up and dragged me over to the concrete slab that was the centerpiece of the room. I was screaming and fighting to get away but panic was draining the energy out of me. I didn't want to feel what was about to happen to me and worked as hard as I could to escape my body. I dissociated and found myself looking down at the horror and not registering the pain.

The same six hooded men who were always part of these rituals were standing around me, and chanting in unison. The man by my feet held up a pointed silver object that was wet with blood that I knew was mine. I had felt him poke it inside my body. He chanted something and walked closer to me, as the man near my head grabbed my chin to open my mouth. I was terrified, watching the hooded man come towards me, my blood glistening on the silver object, knowing that they wanted me to taste it.

The ritual became more frenzied as each man took a turn pouring something wet and oily over me. When it was over and I found myself coming back into my body, I remember looking to the left at the stairs we had come down a couple of hours earlier. I was trying to make sense of where I was. This was a place of worship where people were supposed to be protected, and where God answered prayers.

35

I had reached my tolerance for grown men abusing me in terribly cruel ways. I had simply run out of explanations for the reality that was my life. As a child, I didn't have the reasoning to know that bad things weren't happening to me because I was flawed. I felt abandoned and hopeless. In the basement of that temple I decided that God hated me.

When the ritual was over, everyone left the room except for a man who helped me off the cement block. I had trouble walking. I was in a lot of pain and felt lightheaded. He left me alone as I got dressed to go home. I hated this part. I wasn't allowed to sit and cry, or to pull myself together. I had to get dressed, and out to the car for a ride home with either my mother or my father. My feelings of shame, humiliation and confusion were solidifying. I questioned if I had somehow been complicit in all of this. But that wasn't the case at all. Once again, I had been delivered by my parents to be horribly abused.

When we got home I ran upstairs and shut myself in my room. I turned on a heavy-metal rock album and listened to the same song over, and over again. The angry music from my record player helped me settle down and eventually fall asleep.

When I took a shower the next morning, I was sore and in pain. I was afraid to think of how bruised I would be, and glad that the bruises would be hidden under my clothes. I was a tangled knot of emotions when I got to school and decided to skip my classes. I walked the several miles from school to Craig's house to hide from the world and get high. I spent the whole week trying to forget about what happened to me that Sunday when the six men celebrated the spring full moon.

The next weekend, I was more than ready to party and forget everything. My friend Leanne and I walked to a neighborhood off the beaten path where we used to hang out. The roads weren't paved there and the whole area was tucked behind some fields. It was so isolated that only people who lived there used those dirt roads.

When we got to the end of the road an older guy in a brown van was talking with the kids we were coming to party with that evening. We were all fourteen to sixteen years old and he was obviously in his late twenties. He told me that he was twenty-six. It was a night of smoking weed; partying with good music and listening to this new guy Bruce in the back of his van. No one seemed to know him. He told us that he was just driving by and decided to party with us. We didn't care. He had a van, good music, and weed and that was all that mattered to us.

As the night wore on, Bruce and I began to talk alone in the front seat. I was comfortable talking to him because he was Craig's age. Cindy, a girl who lived down the street where we were partying, came out of her house anxious and upset. She pulled Leanne and I aside and told us that Bruce had raped her the night before. For some reason I didn't believe her and neither did Leanne.

Instead, we looked at her and asked, "Why are you here if he did that to you? Shouldn't you be inside your house? Why would you risk coming out to talk to us if he did that to you?" She got more upset and ran back into her house. The doubting questions we threw at her haunt me to this day.

Even though Leanne and I dismissed Cindy's warning that this man who came out of nowhere was dangerous, we were spooked enough to want to leave the party. Without saying goodbye to anyone we left and walked back home. As we were walking Leanne told me that Cindy was overly dramatic because her parents were getting a divorce. But something inside me had been triggered. I was on high-alert and hyper-vigilant, jumping at every set of headlights that passed by us on our way home. I kept telling myself I was tired and paranoid from too much partying.

The next day was Saturday and I couldn't wait to get out of the house. I had no plan as I left home, but assumed I would find somebody to hang out with before partying again that night. About a half a block to the left of my house was one of the main roads through Sheridan. I was surprised to see Bruce's brown van parked on the side of the road.

He called my name and I walked over to him. He asked if I wanted to go get high. Because I had nowhere in particular to go, I got into his van. My sense of safety was already so compromised at the age of fourteen that I didn't think twice. He drove around the back of our neighborhood where it was swampy and woodsy, and parked. We went into the back of his van and began to smoke. He wore a leather strap on his wrist that said "Smith" on it. I asked if that was his last name and he said, "Yes."

He put his joint down and moved in towards me. I thought he was trying to kiss me and I moved backwards. I didn't want this older guy to be my first kiss. But he wasn't trying to kiss me; he grabbed me and pushed me down on the floor. I couldn't believe this was happening. My brain was so confused. I think a part of me knew what was happening, but this wasn't an organized ritual with a room full of men. It was the guy I had partied with the night before. This must have been what Cindy was trying to tell us happened to her.

He was putting all his weight on my shoulders. I was struggling and telling him to get off of me, but I could tell this was a fight I couldn't win. I could feel my heart pounding and my stomach roil as panic set in and fear overtook my brain. I was still really sore and bruised from what happened six days ago and started to cry. When he was done, he got off me and said, "Get dressed. We're done here."

I was stunned and in terrible pain. I had no real idea what happened or why. He drove me back to my house, and told me to get out of the van. He said something vague, that he had done what he was supposed to do, and again told me get out. I don't know how I managed to get out and walk to my house. My legs felt like rubber. I didn't dissociate when Bruce raped me. I remember it clearly; that trauma is etched deeply into my memory.

Two months after my 15th birthday, I learned I was pregnant. Leanne told me she noticed I had a bump under my shirt and asked if I was late for my period. I had no idea what she was talking about. I had no idea that periods and pregnancy went together. I had no idea that sex could lead to pregnancy. I was totally stunted in knowing how my own body and biology worked. I knew what happened to other girls, but I didn't think of myself as a girl. I didn't think of myself as anything. I had no sense of self and no connection to my body. I only knew how to leave my body when somebody was hurting me.

I realized that I hadn't had a period since before school was out, so Leanne and her boyfriend drove me to the free clinic. I was examined and told I was five months pregnant. They told me it was too late to have an abortion.

Leanne and her boyfriend dropped me off at my house wishing me good luck. I sat on the couch, called for my mother and told her I was five months pregnant. She looked at me with total disgust and shrieked, "How could you do this to me?" She went to the phone and made a call, then told me to go upstairs to my room and never speak to her again. I was grateful to be left alone.

As I lay in my bed that night, I overheard my mother and father talking. They sounded angry and upset, but what hit the hardest was hearing their words about the fastest way to deal with the situation. They had told me they hated me ever since I was a little girl, but that night, I understood perfectly by their tone that they detested me. There were few times in my life when the total lack of love in my childhood really landed hard, and this was one of them.

I felt defeated, afraid and confused. Listening to their conversation, I understood that I had done something wrong and now was going to be punished. I hoped I would just be grounded and ignored. I didn't know what being pregnant meant, so I didn't worry about any next steps. The person at the clinic had told me I couldn't have an abortion. I had no idea that meant I would have to give birth in four months. It honestly never entered my mind. I never thought about the future, because I lived in constant survival mode; waiting for the next atrocity to happen. I didn't worry about the pregnancy that night or the next day. I had repressed the rape and I thought this would disappear too.

Two days later, as I was sitting in class my teacher came and told me that my mother was waiting for me. I had to go home because I was going to the hospital. I was wearing my hair in braids that day and he gently tugged on one and asked me if I was going to be okay. I looked at him confused and said, "I'm not even sick, so why am I going to the hospital?" I'm sure he knew what was going on because I was tiny and I was starting to show. I was so disconnected from my body that I didn't even see myself in a mirror.

When I got into the car with my mother, I asked her twice why I was going to the hospital. The first time she was silent and the second time, she said, "Don't be stupid." Oddly, I remember the shirt I had on at school that day. It was one of my favorites, with soft blues and pinks. As we got closer to the house my nerves got the best of me. When we pulled into the driveway, I opened the car door, flew into the house running for the bathroom to throw-up. In the process, I got some vomit on my beloved shirt. My mother began yelling at me to hurry up; so I took off my shirt, and threw it down the laundry chute. I never wore it again.

My mother walked me to the hospital desk, registered me, took me to a changing room and left. I still had no idea what was happening but by now I surmised it was about being pregnant. A nurse came in and told me to change into a gown. Panic set in. Being told to take off my clothes was always the start of something horrible.

I took off my clothes and put them in the bag. The nurse came back and walked me to a small exam room. She told me to get on the table and put my feet in the stirrups. I didn't know what stirrups were and was not going to listen to her. I said, "No, I'm not going to put my feet in those things. I don't have any clothes on underneath this gown."

She looked at me as if I was from Mars. I was obviously pregnant and she probably assumed I had already been examined to be admitted for this procedure. She told me to just lie down and the doctor would be with me in a few minutes.

I didn't lie down but the doctor did come in a few minutes later. I instantly recognized him. He was part of my father's secret group and one of the men from the spring ritual at the temple. I panicked and started to get off the table. I knew better then to identify him, but I still had no intention of letting him assault me again.

There were two nurses in the room with him. When I started to get off the table they grabbed my arms and held me down. The doctor put my feet in the stirrups, and a third nurse came in and helped hold me down. I was struggling and fighting as hard as I could, like a trapped animal. My mind was exploding in confusion. The nurse who was across the middle of my body kept scolding me to settle down. No one would tell me what was going on. I was terrified. Every instinct told me to get out of there. They must have given me a sedative because eventually I relaxed enough for the nurses to loosen their grip. The procedure began.

The doctor told me he was inserting various size needles inside my body. I began to sob from the pain. I'm not sure how much pain I really felt, because my fear amplified the size and scrape of the instruments he was using. When he was done, he left the room. The nurses stayed with me as I lay there sobbing. To this day, I can still see the procedure room, the lights, the nurses, and the doctor. I can feel the overwhelming fear that gripped my body. I still didn't know what was happening or why I had to stay in the hospital. I did know that I had been humiliated and objectified again. I felt like the gross disgusting pig my father had often told me I was.

A few hours after the procedure, I started feeling cramps. They were worse than any period cramps I had experienced and I had no idea what was happening. My mother came in for a few minutes after they brought me to the room, but for the majority of the day, into the evening I was alone. The nurses weren't talking to me. I felt as if they were treating me like an untouchable creature. They spoke to me curtly and never met my eyes. I heard one of the nurses in the hall say to another, "She is only fifteen." I felt myself flush with embarrassment hearing them talk about me.

Sometime during the night the cramps got much worse. I thought I had peed in the bed and started screaming. There was so much water. My body was locked down with pain, keeping me from getting out of the wet bed. I was terrified and screaming, "What's happening to me?" A nurse came in and told me my water broke, and that the baby would be coming soon. I had *no* idea what that meant and started to cry, writhing in pain as the contractions got worse.

The nurse got me out of bed, changed the sheets, gave me a clean gown and had me lay back down. They examined me and told me that it was time to go to the delivery room. I didn't want to have a baby and I didn't want to go to a delivery room. I was petrified as they wheeled me down the hall, watching the bright lights on the hospital ceiling whoosh by as they pushed the gurney through the double doors.

The delivery room was startling. It was freezing and seemed empty except for a bed. Everyone there wore masks over their faces and gloves. I felt like I was in a horror movie, with masked monsters ready to take out my organs. After all the bizarre and terrifying places I had already been in my young life, I was feeling a new level of confusion, panic and pain.

They moved me to the table, took off my gown, covered me with some sheets and strapped both my arms down on boards, putting an IV in my left arm and a blood pressure cuff on my right. The pain was intense, and I was screaming; I felt as if I was floating and woozy at the same time. The doctor came in and told me that I was ready to have the baby. I don't remember much after that. I believe I heard the doctor tell the nurse standing next to him, that it was a boy. I remember thinking I don't hear a baby crying. I put it all together and concluded they had killed the baby during the procedure the day before, and I had been forced to give birth to him. At that point I must have fallen asleep because I don't remember anything until the next day.

I woke up feeling incredibly sore and sick. My mother was in the room waiting to take me home and the nurse was giving her instructions. I asked the nurse if I could get up to go to the bathroom. I still had an IV in my arm, so the nurse helped me out of bed and told me how to roll the pole along side of me. She let go of my arm and the room faded to black. I had passed out. When I came to, the nurse was taking the IV out of my arm and then helped me to the bathroom. My mother kept going on about how mortified she was that I brought the IV pole down, and how embarrassing that was for her. I felt miserable, confused and just wanted to go home.

When I was released from the hospital, my mother told me to keep my mouth shut about what happened. I was to never tell anyone. She said that my brother Thomas had asked my father where I was. My father told him that I was in the hospital because I had had some female problems. My sister had called home the night before I was released. Lucy and I sounded so similar on the phone that my mother asked her why I was calling from the hospital so late at night. That was how Lucy found out. She didn't believe I had female problems and grilled my mother until she was told some version of the truth. My oldest brother Adam never knew I was in the hospital. He was long gone and rarely made contact with the family.

When my father came home from work that night he refused to look at me. In fact for the next three months I lived in our house ignored by my parents. I was again, like so many times in the past, invisible. The only time my mother acknowledged what had happened to me was when she had to take me to a follow-up visit. It was the fastest doctor's visit I ever had. The doctor was in and out of the room quickly, but I made sure to keep my eyes on his. I was never going to look away from any of my abusers again.

I never had to endure another seasonal ritual after that spring of 1974 and Bruce Smith disappeared as quickly as he came. But I am still triggered when spring approaches every year. The warmer days, the evening chill, and the full moons remind me of the time I realized that God hated me, of the man in a brown van, and of a baby who I would never know.

Chapter 7
WHERE IS MINNESOTA

My father was diagnosed with leukemia when I was fifteen years old. He tried some alternative treatment in Ontario but it became apparent that it wasn't working. A year later, he began to plan around the inevitable fact that he was going to die. He traveled overseas one more time, resigned from those assignments and focused on his engineering company that he had recently sold to a Minnesota firm. I knew what was going on peripherally, but I hadn't had a real conversation with my parents since my forced abortion the year before.

I came home one day after school to find my parents and Rabbi Samuel in the living room having a serious conversation. It was an odd time of day for my father to be home and the room felt heavy and somber. When they looked up and saw me, my parents said they had decided to sell their house and move to Minnesota. They said I had a choice. I could move with them or stay with Rabbi Samuel and finish high school.

I was stunned. Both options were intolerable. Do I move to a new state where I didn't know anyone, or stay with one of the men who participated in the ritual ceremonies? I was sure I didn't want to stay with the rabbi, but I also didn't know anything about Minnesota. In fact, I'm sure I had no idea where it even was on a map. I was torn about what to do, but the thought of living with that man seemed more unbearable than moving with my parents. They were known quantities. Besides I knew my father was dying and I had mixed emotions over what that meant for me and how life would look after he died.

I made the decision to move with them, thinking they would wait until I was done with the school year and move during the summer. But they wanted to move as soon as possible. My father's business partner had already relocated to Minnesota and they had a big contract. Time was running out for my father to be well enough to work. My parents took several trips to Minnesota to find a new house. I don't remember anything about their selling, packing up, or moving. It's a blank to me, as if it never happened; I simply have no memory of it at all.

I stayed home alone while my parents house-hunted in Minnesota. I had accepted that I was moving away from my friends and felt sad, but I told people it was a chance to start over and have a new adventure. The only one I shared my fear of moving with was my closest friend Ann. Her house was the place I went to for respite every weekend. Ann's parents and brothers loved one another, and they made me feel at home whenever I was there. Like most kids, my friends and I dreamed about moving away from the place we grew up in, to see the world. At parties, I became the girl who was actually going to do that. The excitement from others helped me keep my outward appearance upbeat.

My brothers both lived in Grant but I seldom saw them. We were siblings who had no relationship to one another. As soon as each of them turned eighteen, my brothers and sister left home and seldom returned. I was only sixteen when my parents decided to move, still two years away from the freedom that my siblings enjoyed.

When my brothers found out my parents were moving, neither one of them offered to let me stay with them to finish out the school year. Their rejection stung, but I acted as if it didn't matter. I'd come to accept that my family honestly didn't care about what happened to me, but their abandonment was still a crushing blow. I had more feelings than ever to deny.

I fell into a deep depression. I was numb and emotionally shut down during those last months in Michigan. I built a thick wall between myself and the outside world. Even though I had the ability to dissociate, the traumatic events of my life were having a cumulative effect on my psychological and emotional wellbeing.

A few months before my junior year ended my parents moved and left me alone. They made no arrangements for my care. I asked friends if I could stay with them and every family said yes, and took me into their home. My own parents never spoke to them or offered anything for feeding or sheltering me. I moved from one friend's house to the next, feeling abandoned and afraid, grateful I had a place to sleep every night.

The night before I finally left for Minnesota, Ann and I went to a huge party out in some fields. There were kegs of beer, lots of weed and rock music blasting from car speakers. I remember telling someone I was moving to Minnesota the next day. She looked at me and said, "Oh yeah? That's where Mary Tyler Moore lives. You'll meet your husband there someday." I remember that moment as if it were yesterday. By the time I was ten years old, I had stopped wishing, and hoping or dreaming for anything, and here was a total stranger dreamily predicting a happy future for me.

The next morning, on my 17th birthday, I stood waiting at the end of Ann's driveway for my brother to pick me up. She and I hugged good-bye, I promised to write, and got into Thomas' car to start the fifteen hour drive. I had never spent much time with my oldest brother and I don't think we had ever said more than a few words to each other. I expected a long and uncomfortable drive. We were virtual strangers driving toward the parents who had made both of our lives unthinkably miserable.

I remember two things about the trip. First, I remember Thomas yelling at me to shut-up when I sang along to the radio, and second, his car breaking down in some small town. He called my mother from a pay phone, and I could hear them yelling at each other about who was going to pay for the repairs. Everything else about the drive is a blur of small towns and freeways.

Even though I was spiraling into a deep depression before I left, the long drive stirred a small hope in me. Moving to a new place where no one knew me was appealing. Maybe I could leave my life behind and become someone else, someone who hadn't survived seventeen years of hell. But when Thomas delivered me to my parents at their new house, I realized nothing had changed but the address.

Chapter 8
WILLOW LAKE

I was shocked when we arrived at my parent's new home. It felt out in the middle of nowhere. Their townhouse complex felt isolated, tucked into the woods in a mostly undeveloped area. The house was brand new with plush carpets and chandeliers throughout. Their backyard was wooded and just beyond those woods, were college athletic fields.

After a frosty and argumentative greeting between Thomas and my mother, I decided to explore the house and found my new bedroom upstairs. It was the biggest bedroom I'd ever had. It had thick blue carpet that hugged my feet with each step, three closets and large windows. I loved my room instantly and I knew it would make a fine refuge. And it did, for a while.

My brother flew back to Michigan the next morning. I wouldn't talk with Thomas again until a year later. That was when my father lay dying and all four of us siblings would sit in a vigil for five days. The week after I arrived, my mother drove me to my new high school. It was unlike any school I had ever seen, a low sprawling building with almost no walls. The office was walled off, but the classrooms had no walls or doors, just partitions reaching halfway up to the ceiling. There was a traditional high school on the other side of Willow Lake, but Southside High was a new concept the city was trying out. It was a school without walls, where classes were measured in modules not hours.

I met with my counselor Mr. Franklin that first day, to talk about what classes I needed to graduate. It turned out I had taken all my required classes in Michigan so I could spend the year taking electives. That was fine with me, so I chose classes like "I'm OK, You're OK," Pop Culture, Typing, History and OJT (On the Job Training). They placed me in the secretarial program and gave me a job in the Media Center at school. Mr. Franklin wished me good luck and invited me to come and see him when school started if I had any questions.

My depression deepened after I moved. I spent my days in my room sleeping and listening to records. I had no interest in meeting anyone nor did I have the self-esteem to think anyone would want to meet me. This was before cell phones or email, and my parents wouldn't pay for long distance calls. At first my friends and I would write back and forth daily, but senior year started for all of us and the letters slowed down considerably.

Those first days of school were awful. I had come from a large suburb where high schools were populated by the blending of several junior highs. It was common to make new friends every school year, with kids merging in and out of groups from different parts of the city. In Willow Lake, everyone knew each other from elementary school and church. Everyone was white, with blond hair and blue eyes. Everyone looked the same and they all had Minnesota accents. There was no diversity, no music, nothing to do. I felt like an alien dropped into a small town where outsiders were not welcome. I also realized that by senior year everyone was comfortable in their clique and just waiting to finish high school. I was the new kid, a small curiosity for both guys and girls, but it was hard to break into and be accepted by any group.

A couple of weeks after school started, I got a note to meet with Mr. Franklin. I hadn't given him a second thought since I picked out my class schedule and couldn't imagine what he wanted. The less contact I had with adults the better I felt. My first few weeks in Minnesota had given me a much needed respite from my life in Michigan.

When I got to Mr. Franklin's office he asked me the usual questions about how school was going. Did I like my classes? Was I finding my way around, and were the students friendly? I answered him quickly and cheerfully saying, "Everything is fine." But I could feel my heart pounding in my chest. I wondered how long I had to be alone with this person and why he really wanted to talk to me. He told me to stop by again soon. I knew I wouldn't do that, but told him okay and left.

I made a couple of friends to eat lunch with and my classes were going well. But I was failing miserably in my secretarial OJT job in the Media Center. I couldn't concentrate on the typing. I didn't care about the letters, or how many times the frustrated secretary would have me retype some correspondence because of my typing errors. I met a few of the boys whose job it was to put the projectors and movies away and found I had a much better time talking to them than typing.

One day, after the secretary had me retype the same letter three times, my boss called me into his office and asked me if I liked my job. I said, "No, I hate working here and I hate this school." He sent me to the principal's office and the principal sent me to my counselor. That's how I ended up talking with Mr. Franklin almost daily for the next nine months, and how he became a part of my life until the day I got married.

The first thing he did was set me up in a volunteer position helping children with severe disabilities in their group home. He took me out of OJT, but arranged early release so I could get out of school after my classes were done in the morning. He told me that before I went home every day, I needed to stop by his office and check in with him.

There was something about the way he took charge with my school schedule and gave me direction to come talk to him that felt safe. I didn't feel handled like I had by every adult in my life up to that point. What I felt, for the first time, was that someone was taking care of me. He didn't address the issue of my hating school; he was more interested in the task at hand. That was, changing my schedule, finding me another job, and making sure I promised to touch base with him. He would address the misery I was feeling at a later time.

I stopped by his office every day to check in. There were a lot of times that I spent hours just hanging out there when he didn't have other appointments. It was the only place I felt a sense of safety. During school breaks he stayed in touch with me by phone, checking in, asking me how I was doing, and telling me that he cared. He didn't push too hard when he asked questions that I clearly struggled with answering in a coherent way. I would abruptly change the subject remembering the warnings I was given not to tell anyone, anything that had happened to me.

When my father's leukemia progressed and he needed blood transfusions, Mr. Franklin and one of the science teachers encouraged the teaching staff to go the hospital and see if they were a match for transfusions. Mr. Franklin interjected himself in ways that supported me and made my life easier during that year. It was my senior year. I was new to the state and school, my father was dying. I was clearly an abused and neglected kid, and I was extremely depressed. He recognized my distress and gave me adult support.

We stayed in touch after I graduated. He wanted to make sure I knew he was there for me, just like he was there for his own children. If too many weeks passed before I checked in, he would call me and arrange to meet for breakfast. When I started using diet pills to suppress my appetite and give me the energy to work two jobs, Mr. Franklin counseled me about the slippery slope of drug use. After our breakfasts, he would make me promise to eat and get some sleep until we met again.

One of those breakfasts was a few weeks before I went on my first trip to the Middle East. I was moody and insecure that morning. When we got to our cars and stopped for our usual goodbye hug, he held me tight and told me he loved me. I was nineteen years old and it was the first time in my life someone had said those words to me. I knew he meant it in a fatherly way, but most importantly I knew he meant it. I didn't tell him I loved him back; I had never said those words in my life, nor had attached to someone enough to feel that emotion. I think he knew I loved him. If he didn't that day, he did when he showed up at my wedding reception four years later.

My life changed drastically when I came home from the Middle East. I left behind all of my past including Mr. Franklin. But when I sat down to send out my wedding invitations he was the first one on my list. I didn't know if he would remember me or even want to come to my wedding. I just knew that he was the most important person for me to invite.

I was standing with a group of people at our wedding reception, when I happened to look up and see him. It was the perfect moment. I couldn't believe my eyes when I saw him walking toward me. It was as if the whole world stopped and it was just Mr. Franklin and I on the lawn that October afternoon. Hugging him, crying, and thanking him for coming, I felt that same love and support he had given me a few years before.

He didn't want to mingle with, or talk to anyone; he said he was there just for me. We stood off to the side and talked for about 45 minutes. At one point my new husband Jay came up to meet him, but then left us alone and entertained our guests. I knew as we were winding down the conversation that this would be the last time I would see Mr. Franklin. My life had changed drastically and I knew I had to protect him at all costs. Before he left, I told him I loved him and he told me he loved me. He looked at me and told me I was beautiful, and I could feel the fatherly pride he had for me. It was a bittersweet moment.

Mr. Franklin is ever present in my heart and will remain there until the day I die. I'll never forget the high school counselor who probably, on more than one occasion, risked his job to save a lost girl from Michigan.

For many, many reasons I'm glad I moved to the state where Mary Tyler Moore lived. As the girl at the party prophesized, I *did* meet my husband in Minnesota. But most importantly, it was where I heard my first, "I Love You" from an adult who wanted nothing more than to keep me safe, and healthy, and to show me I was worthy of fatherly love.

Chapter 9
MARCH

It would be interesting to have each of my siblings describe their experience of the week that my father died. It was the first time since my sister's wedding ten years earlier, that all four of us were together for any length of time. And yet, there we were, keeping a five-day vigil at my father's hospital bedside.

It was fascinating and frightening to watch my father move through the stages of dying. He was quite lucid as he called each one of us to his bedside and asked permission to die. He didn't ask for forgiveness, or apologize for hurting us; he just wanted permission to die. As the doses of morphine increased he began to go in and out of consciousness. He was seeing and talking to his deceased family and his beloved cat. These were all ghosts to us, but they were real and comforting to him. For two days before he died he held conversations with his mother, who had been killed in the war when he was seventeen years old. Eventually, he spoke only in Hungarian, his first language.

He struggled to die. Part of that may have been the morphine, but he seemed to have a need for closure with certain people before he could let go. The day before his death, a steady stream of people came and went, said their goodbyes, and he fell into a deep sleep.

Once he drifted into that sleep state, we were told that he would probably die within a few hours. We opted to stay in the hospital that night and wait. Each of us was dealing with our father's death in our own way, and nobody was talking to or comforting one another.

Once a year while we were growing up, my father had made us sit in a line on the couch and recite, "See no evil, hear no evil, speak no evil" while he took pictures. Waiting for word of his death we seemed to be recreating those moments, sitting in a row staring blankly into space.

My sister Lucy loved my father with all her heart. He was always her daddy, and she was grief-stricken that he was dying. She spent a lot of time in his room feeling an otherworldly connection to him and reporting many sightings of his mother. My brother, Thomas was filled with guilt for never living up to the rigid standards that my father had so often reinforced with his fist. Thomas' mix of guilt and grief was making him angry and contentious. Adam hated my father too. He could never live up to the impossible standards that had been expected of him either. He was distant and off in his own world; silent and withdrawn.

I felt a lot of ambivalence about my father dying. I had watched him struggle with three rounds of chemotherapy and had seen the disease ravage this once very powerful man. I didn't want him to suffer any longer, but at the same time his suffering was the only restitution I would ever extract from this man who had abused me since I was a baby.

When I moved to Minnesota, he and I had spent countless hours together. He taught and then quizzed me for hours about national and international politics. He spent a lot of time telling me his life story. He seemed anxious for me to learn his past so that he wouldn't be forgotten by his future grandchildren. My father's entire family was killed in the Holocaust and he carried immense survivor's guilt. It was confusing for me. He was unbelievably abusive to me and yet I felt compassion and respect for his life story. I would have preferred to feel a neat and clean hatred and disgust towards him.

Early the next morning, the rabbi on the hospice team came into the room to talk to the four of us. Rabbi Lyon had spent many hours talking with and comforting my father during his extended hospital stays. The four of us siblings were exhausted from lack of sleep and the endless waiting. The air was heavy with grief, confusion, and boredom. The rabbi told us he wanted to relay a few words from my father to each of us. I had an instant distrust of this man when I met him, and that day, chills ran down my spine when he began to speak.

He stopped first in front of my brothers and told them that my father loved them very much. He knelt down to my grieving sister, took her hands into his and began telling her how much my father loved her, how much my father spoke of her and that he himself would be there for her in her grief.

Then he walked over to me and without a moment's hesitation said, "You are our tough little shit, and you will be fine." He walked away. I felt three things simultaneously: hurt, rejected, and a profound sense of dread.

The next morning, my father's nurse Kathy called us into his room. She said it was time. We all gathered around his bed. My mother was weeping, the rabbi was reading prayers, his nurse and my sister were crying, and my brothers and I were staring at him, watching him take his last breaths.

When he died, all I wanted was to get out of his room. As I turned to walk out, Kathy grabbed my arm and told me I had to stay, she pointed in the corner of the room and said, "Look, there he is." It was hardly comforting for me to imagine him hovering over us. I wanted him to be gone, not become a ghost who could watch me from beyond.

I have no memory of driving home from the hospital that day. My next real memory was of later that night. I was laying on one of the beds in my room just staring out the window, while my sister was on the other bed sobbing with uncontrollable grief. My mother walked by the bedroom, heard my sister crying, poked her head inside and said, "He was *my* husband, he was *just* your father, I don't know what you're *so* upset about." I was stunned; even as nasty and narcissistic as my mother was, this was a new low for her. As soon as she huffed out of the room, I knew the comment she hurled at my sister would forever cost her having any future relationship with Lucy.

In the Jewish tradition, it's customary that a person be buried within 24 hours of their death. I expected the funeral to be the following day because I knew arrangements had been made, and the rabbi from the hospital was going to do the service. But when I woke up the next morning, my mother told me that Rabbi Samuel from Grant as well as many others from out-of- town were traveling to the funeral. The service would be postponed for a day. I asked her why the rabbi was coming from Grant since we already had one to do the service, and she told me that actually three rabbis were going to speak at the service, but that Rabbi Samuel was coming for me.

The last time I had seen him was two years earlier when I walked into my parent's house and was told they were moving to Minnesota. I thought I'd never have to see him or any of my abusers from Michigan again.

Hearing these funeral plans from my mother, I felt an enormous need to escape. I told my sister I was going to the mall and asked her if she wanted to come with me. I was really stressed that I didn't own any black clothes and needed to go shopping for funeral outfits. I didn't tell her I was terrified about Rabbi Samuel coming. I kept the secrets about the years he participated in the rituals. I knew I had to stay silent; I had always kept silent.

A large group of out-of-town people gathered in my mother's living room on the day of the funeral. I hadn't been around this many people from my past in a very long time. There were old neighbors, my grandparents, and the rabbi from Grant. I was sick to my stomach. I spent most of the morning throwing up from the stress and fear. I was flashing between Michigan and Minnesota. I couldn't process how my Michigan abusers had found me in Minnesota. I thought I'd left that part of my life behind. How could they have followed me here?

Everything around me seemed surreal as we drove to the service. I felt like I was in a trance walking into the funeral home. We were led into a room where the family waits to make their entrance after all the guests are seated. It was all so strange. I saw many people my parents knew, but I also saw new friends of mine. I had called my friend Mary and told her that my father had died. She had in turn, called some other friends and they all came to the funeral. I remember thinking how strange it was that these nice kids were sitting with all these vicious adults.

Three rabbis eulogized my father that day. One was from the temple my parents joined when they moved to Minnesota, one was the rabbi that I met at the hospital, and the last one was Rabbi Samuel from Grant. I have no idea what they said, although I do remember someone speaking of Max's children and hearing my sister burst into sobs. I hadn't shed any tears; not at the hospital, not at home, and not at the funeral. Thinking back, I never have shed those tears.

After the funeral everyone was told to follow the hearse to the cemetery. I stood on the sidewalk by myself and watched my family get into the cars and drive away. I stood there like a statue, frozen, not knowing where to go or what to do. Our neighbor from Michigan came over to me, gently grabbed my arm and helped me into their car to drive me to the gravesite. I remember it was cold outside and that my shoes were getting wet, but I don't remember anything else until we were home and welcoming the mourners and rabbis to our house for the after-funeral luncheon.

A few minutes after we got home from the service, the phone rang and my sister told me it was Mr. Franklin calling for me. Wanting privacy, I ran upstairs to my bedroom to take the call. He had heard about my father's death and wanted to come to the house to support me. I really needed him there, but when he asked for the address, my insides wound tight with fear and panic. I knew the people gathered downstairs weren't safe and I didn't want him in danger. I didn't have any idea what that meant, but I felt I had to protect him at any cost. So, instead of giving him the address, I just hung up on him. I stood there looking at the phone feeling both relieved and appalled at myself for being so rude. I sat down wearily on my sister's bed and heard a knock on the bedroom door.

Rabbi Samuel was suddenly in my room. He sat down next to me on the bed, and I noticed he had a copy of Caddish, the Jewish prayer for the dead in his hands. He asked me if I wanted him to transliterate it for me. He was sitting too close and I was feeling anxious. Something felt off and I was starting to panic. I told myself to keep focused on his pretty blue shirt.

All at once his tone changed. He put his arm tightly around me. His voice got quiet and stern. He said, "You belong to us. The next part of your life begins today." It happened so fast. One minute he was talking to me about a prayer for the dead; the next minute he had his hands on me. He whispered threats in my left ear. I was shaken. I didn't understand what just happened or why? My body was shaking from the shock of his grip and my mind was spinning out of control. I was trying to sob and keep quiet at the same time. My brain felt like it was exploding, trying to comprehend what all this meant.

After a few moments I did what I always did when I got hurt and my abuser walked away. I pulled myself together, brushed my hair and went downstairs to the group of mourners. It wouldn't be long before I understood what Rabbi Samuel had meant.

Chapter 10
CHANGE IS COMING

My siblings and all the out-of-town visitors left within a few days of the funeral. Two weeks after my father's death, my mother announced that she was leaving for Alaska. When I asked her what I was supposed to do while she was gone she became enraged, screaming at me, "My husband just died so I need to get away from everything." She yelled about how selfish and cruel I was, and how dare I question her need to get away from the house.

Two days later, she got on a plane and flew off to Alaska. She left me with no money, no numbers to call in case of emergency, and no information on how to get in touch with her.

I called my friend Mary to tell her that my mother was going out of town, and Mary was furious. She had told me how sad she was that my father had died, and how she had been hugging her own dad a lot because she couldn't imagine how painful it would be to lose him. I told her how scared I was to be in the house alone and asked her if she could stay with me for a couple of days. The house was too cold, quiet, and empty and at the same time, felt full of ghosts. I was scared to be alone in there, and I wanted nothing to do with my room where the rabbi had threatened me.

I was so grateful Mary came to stay with me. We invited a couple of boys over to party the first night she was there. I was still trying to deal with my father's death, the threat from the rabbi, and my mother leaving me alone with no way to reach her. I was also operating on very little sleep and felt panicky every time I had to go into my room for fresh clothes. I couldn't imagine sleeping in there and I never imagined bringing a boy up into my room. But as the night grew long and expectations heavier, I found myself bringing one of the boys upstairs. With each step toward my room, I felt more agitated. We moved close to my bed and he bent over to kiss me. I panicked and lashed out. I started screaming at him not to touch me. I was having a terrible flashback, getting him mixed up with the rabbi, only this time I was fighting back and running away.

I ran out of the room, slammed the door, and ran down two flights of stairs to the basement where Mary and her date were. I screamed at her that I had to protect us. I pulled her up off the couch and pushed both of us into the small bathroom, locking the door behind us.

I was crying hysterically. Mary was stunned and trying to get me to tell her what had happened. She told me to wait a minute and left the bathroom. She told her date to leave with the guy I had left in my bedroom and then came back. She closed the bathroom door and waited until I settled down, and finally convinced me that we were safe.

I scared Mary that night. More than 30 years later she still remembers that night clearly. She knew then that my fear and panic were way out of proportion. I had known this boy for months. He wasn't a threat nor was I uncomfortable with him. Mary was also just eighteen at the time, and was very confused. I couldn't tell her about what happened at my father's funeral, and I also couldn't tell her about my childhood in Michigan. I knew better than to tell anyone about my childhood.

Mary spent the next two nights with me before she had to go back home. I remember her commenting that there was nothing to eat in the house. My mother left me with no food and no money to get groceries. I didn't care about food, because by then I was working a few days a week at a group home. I knew that I could eat with the residents there.

The night my mother was supposed to arrive at the airport, I asked Mary to come with me to pick her up. I'd never driven out to the airport and I was nervous, especially since she was landing so late at night. Mary couldn't go, so I ventured out alone. I found her flight and stood waiting at the gate for her to deplane. She never got off. I waited until the next flight came, and the one after that, but no mother. By then it was 2 a.m. and I had been at the airport for four hours. I felt frightened when she didn't arrive and abandoned because I thought she didn't want to come home.

I left the airport, found my car, and headed home hoping that maybe I had missed her and she was already at home. She would be angry, but she would be there and I wouldn't be alone in that house any longer. She wasn't home, so I just lay on the couch waiting for the sun to come up, and to figure out what I should do next.

Thinking I went to the airport on the wrong day, I went back the following night. This time, I didn't stay until 2 a.m., but I must have looked just as forlorn and miserable as I did the night before waiting for a passenger that didn't arrive. When I got home, I told myself she probably wasn't coming back, but I would figure out what to do in the morning.

The next day, I got a nasty phone call from my mother, asking me why I wasn't at the airport. When I told her I had come two nights in a row to pick her up, she called me stupid and launched into a tirade. How could I leave her stranded at the airport? She was exhausted from her trip. What kind of person would do such a thing? As she continued her diatribe, she admitted that her flights had changed. She was indeed home two days later than originally planned. All the way home from the airport, I listened to her huff and puff and sigh, but at least I knew I wasn't crazy. I had gone to the airport on the right night to pick her up. She just hadn't bothered to tell me her plans had changed.

She traveled quite a bit the first few months after my father died. After her first trip to the Middle East, she was consumed with the notion of immigrating there. When she was in town, there were times at night that I would hear a familiar Hungarian accent coming from her room. When I asked who was talking to her, she told me I was hearing things. I began to think I was hearing my dead father come back at night to talk to my mother. It wasn't until she told me she was moving to the Middle East to be near my father's best friend, Ron, that I figured out she was listening to tapes he was mailing to her. I don't know why she didn't tell me about the tapes in the first place. I'm not sure why it was easier for her to let me think I was crazy then to tell me the truth.

As soon as I turned eighteen I began looking for a roommate so I could move away from my mother. I had been spreading the word at work, and finally a golden opportunity came my way. One of my co-workers was looking for a roommate to move in with her in June.

It was wonderful news to me and I was feeling elated when I came home to tell my mother that I was moving out. Finally, like my three siblings, I was going to escape. Even though she had been talking about selling the house and moving to the Middle East within the year, she exploded and began screaming at me that her children hated her and no one cared what happens to her. She shrieked, "No one cares whether I live or die, so I may as well move to the other side of the world." Even though she was speaking the truth, I was hurt and angry that she was going to use my moving out as a way to martyr herself to anyone who would listen. I would again look like the heartless, cruel, and evil daughter she portrayed me to be.

Soon after I settled into my new apartment, landed a second job, adopted a cat and was feeling a wonderful sense of freedom, I received a call from Rabbi Lyon. My mother had given him my number, and he asked if I would meet with him. He told me he knew I was interested in special education and that he knew of a place that I might be interested in touring. I didn't think to say no, or to question why he had me picking him up at his house. I simply agreed to go, got directions, and picked him up the next day.

Everything about the situation was uncomfortable. When I picked him up he told me we were going to the hospital where he worked and told me how to get there. The car ride was heavy with silence. I was on full alert. This was the same person who coldly told me how I was a tough little shit in the hospital. His demeanor in the car was frosty. I was confused because he had called me, I hadn't called him. After a long drive, we pulled up in front of the big ugly brown building that was the state hospital. My mind flashed back to when I was ten years old and the times I had been taken to the facility to be trained.

The air turned electric when I saw the sinister smirk on his face. I looked at him and the building, and panicked. I opened the car door and started running in the opposite direction. I didn't know why I was running or where I thought I was going. I can't tell you why I didn't just drive away in my car. Pure instinct told me to run. The rabbi was much taller than I was so it took him no time at all to catch up with me. He grabbed my arm with a firm grip, turned me around, and told me we were going inside to have a look around.

My heart was thumping hard in my chest as we went through the doors. He showed me the units where the people with developmental disabilities were locked out of sight. It hurt me to see what inhumane conditions these people lived in. This was before state institutions were closed down and people were mainstreamed. Even though I was afraid for myself, I wanted to take each and every one of those people home with me, just so they could experience some kindness.

We came to the floor where the most psychologically disturbed patients were locked away. It smelled of disinfectant and was noisy in a way that unsettled me. The rabbi grabbed my left elbow. He explained how disappointed the people who counted on me for discretion would be, if I should think to run away, or tell anyone about the training that I had been given. He told me that even though I was a tough little shit, I still needed to follow the rules. If I didn't do what was expected of me, I might end up here. He nodded his head toward the locked ward.

The rabbi led me out the door, told me to get in the car and drive us back to his house. I felt confused to the point of shutting down completely. I couldn't begin to understand what he was talking about, but I didn't have the courage to ask, or to openly defy him either. So I dropped him off with his family, and went home to pretend that none of this happened. A few months later, I took my first trip overseas.

PART 2

Chapter 11
THE FIRST TRIP

I felt relieved when my mother decided to move overseas. I'd been living on my own for about a year by then, worked two jobs, and was self-sufficient. She asked me to travel with her to help her on the airplane with her two cats. Even though I didn't want to have anything to do with my mother, I adored those two cats. I couldn't imagine the stress they would be under if they couldn't be with their humans on the flight.

I don't have much recollection of the flights until we arrived at the airport in the Middle East. It was the first time I had gone through customs. The workers went through my luggage and spoke to me in their native language. When I asked someone later why they used their language instead of English, I was told they look for some sort of a sign that you understand what they're saying.

My father's best friend, the man my mother was having an affair with, was at the airport waiting for us. In the airport cafeteria Ron seemed ecstatic that I looked so much like my father. I felt as if he was inspecting a package that has been delivered, rather than just happy to meet me. I was being presented for approval. An eerie feeling crept into my stomach as I was being assessed. He took a couple of pictures out of his front pocket and showed them to me. I didn't hear a word of what he was saying because he sounded exactly like my dead father. Maybe I was beginning to feel the jet-lag. Maybe I was tuning into a deep knowing that there was a sinister person sitting across from me.

It dawned on me that I didn't have my luggage with me. My mother had her luggage beside her, but during all the fuss of meeting Ron and going to the cafeteria, I had forgotten about my bag. We went to the counter and my mother filled out some forms to find my lost luggage. She used my address in the U.S. and not her Middle Eastern one. I felt upset and confused about what she wrote. Why didn't she put her address down?

I recognized that I was exhausted from the flights, from listening to this man who sounded like my father, and hearing my mother speak the local dialect. Maybe she did write down the right address, but that's not what I saw her put down on the sheet of paper. After he assured me that they would find my lost bags, Ron drove us to my mother's new home. I felt jet lagged, the cats were upset, and I just wanted to sleep.

We settled my mother into her beautiful new home by the Mediterranean Sea. It was tucked away in an enclave of gorgeous homes, the likes of which I had only seen in the movies. The sea was directly across her quiet street. I could hear the waves gently crashing onto the shore. The gardens were lush and her front door was beautifully carved.

My luggage finally arrived three days later. It was the same luggage I'd brought with me, but most of my clothes were gone, and replaced with things I had never seen before. I was very upset, and angry. I shouted to anyone in earshot, "Where are my clothes?" My mother told me to shut up and enjoy the new clothes. Why didn't anyone else think it was strange that my luggage reappeared with my things gone and replaced by new clothes in my size? This didn't feel like jet lag, it felt as if the world has started to spin out of control.

I got some rest and my exhaustion faded. We began to travel all around the country. I visited ancient ruins, watched archeological digs, and went to the usual tourist destinations. I enjoyed learning the history of this country and began to understand the struggles the Middle Eastern people had as they tamed this inhospitable land. The first time we traveled to Hellan, I felt intoxicated by the colors, dress, and the mix of ethnicities and cultures co-mingling in the old part of the city. The smells and languages flooded my senses. I was at once overwhelmed and drawn into this ancient city's noise.

There I was introduced to people who were childhood friends of my father. He had immigrated to Canada when he left his birthplace, but many of his friends settled in the Middle East. Time and again the people I met seemed as if they had been expecting me. They seemed very pleased that I looked like my father. Again, I felt as if they were happy that the package that had been delivered was as expected. There was a lot of talk around me, but not directly to me. I felt as if I was being sized up for something but no one was telling me what it was. This felt very uncomfortable, but I told myself that these were just cultural differences.

My mother and I stayed in several different apartments in Hellan. People I'd met would come by to pick me up and take me on tours. One of these people was Daniel, and he took me to the old city. He led me to out-of-the-way nooks and crannies and twisty alleys that were of no interest to me, or probably to any other tourist my age. There was a constant hand on my left elbow and I was called vaguely familiar nick-names such as "Little One" and "Butterfly." I was becoming aware that things were not as they seemed.

Sometime during the first week of my visit I was introduced to a soldier named Gabe. My mother told me that he'd been assigned to be my tour guide. He was in his late twenties and didn't speak English. I wanted nothing to do with him. He seemed creepy to me. The second day we were together he thought that because I was American, I would be open to having sex with him. His line, as he came in for a kiss was, "American girl's fast, yes?"

Gabe toured me around the northern part of the country. He showed me how to cross borders without my passport, and the right etiquette for visiting families that looked as if they were from ancient desert tribes. At one of our stops he had someone take our picture, insisting that I wear his army shirt and hat. I didn't want to put on his foul sweaty clothes, but he insisted. I felt forced to comply, but with an icy feeling shimmying up and down my spine.

On our last day together, Gabe took me to an old military jail that had been turned into a tourist attraction. He seemed stressed and I felt as if I was being taken there for some purpose other than touring. Visiting a jail wasn't remotely interesting to me as a nineteen year old girl. I felt a gnawing fear as we entered one of the cells and saw the iron shackles attached to the bed frame to bind the hands and feet of the prisoners. Gabe put his hand on me and pointed to the chains and said, "See, yes?" Maybe he meant nothing by that statement. Maybe he was just a really creepy older guy trying to impress a teenager, but I intimated a lot from his body language and the way he was looking at me. I nodded in assent and we left. He drove me back to my mother's house and I never saw him again.

My mother took me with her on another trip to Hellan to see Daniel. I didn't want to see him again, the scary man who toured me around the city when we first arrived, touching my left elbow and calling me by those nicknames.

Along the road my mother pulled over to pick up a soldier who looked to be near my age. He'd been standing on the side of the road in his army fatigues with a gun slung over his shoulder. It seemed strange that we pulled over and stopped for him, because we passed a lot of other hitchhikers on the road. She seemed to purposefully pull over and offer him a ride. Was this a rendezvous rather than a random hitchhiker? He immediately started conversing with my mother. I couldn't understand the language but it seemed as if they were talking about something specific; not the chit-chat that I would expect with a hitchhiker. A strange, biting fear began gnawing at my stomach.

It was a few hours' drive to Hellan. By now the hitchhiker had introduced himself as Arik and he went with us as we met up with Daniel. Arik spoke very little English but in spite of that, Daniel assigned him to be my tour guide. My mother encouraged me to go off with Arik. That seemed odd to me. In America, hitchhikers are associated with danger. In spite of my trepidation a part of me felt excited to finally be with someone my own age.

Arik and I took a bus to the old city. He brought me to an old apartment building and we climbed the outside stairs to the roof. He seemed to know where we were going, and was purposeful about climbing up onto that particular roof. Once on top of the roof, I sat down on a large metal housing. I was looking down at my skirt, shirt and sandals feeling awkward about the outfit I was wearing. When we left my mother's house, I didn't know we were going to pick up a guy who was going to take me on a date around the old city. I was fretting about the colors of my skirt and shirt and whether I looked okay, when Arik waved me over to where he was standing. After much cajoling I walked over to the side of the building and looked down at a street that was vacant except for a lone car. There was a sudden flash of light. Arik turned to me, grabbed my arm and hurried us down the stairs. I had no idea why we were rushing down the stairs and into the bustle of the old city, but a few minutes later we were on a bus to continue this very odd date.

Even though the old city was the tourist destination of choice, there was a sprawling modern city outside the ancient walls. There was a large military base located in the middle of the city. Arik led me to the back of the base. We sneaked in through the fence and into the surrounding woods. After some intimate time in the woods, he brought me to the barracks. We hung out with his army buddies who were excited to practice their English with me. I was thrilled with all this attention from guys my age. It was the middle of the night, and I was drunk with the sights, sounds and excitement of being sneaked onto an army base in a foreign country.

I'm sure there are military bases that have security lapses. But looking back on that experience, I was awestruck by the fact that in a city where burned remains of jeeps from recent bombings stood along the road, there was a big enough security breach to allow a young girl to get into a base through a fence, and hang out with the soldiers in their barracks until dawn.

The next morning, Arik dropped me off at Daniel's apartment. Daniel met us at the door and gave Arik a thin but sinister smile. He turned to me and in a cold voice asked, "Do you know what could have happened to you if you had been caught sneaking onto a military base?" I felt the ice again climb up my spine. It wasn't my idea to go to the base, and how did he know where we were all night? Everything inside of me went cold as I felt the power of his presence and began to realize how dangerous Daniel was to me. I didn't explain or defend myself. I looked at the ground feeling small and guilty.

Arik left me at Daniel's so I could eat and get some rest. As I lay down I thought about the last two weeks. Soon I had a pounding headache. I recalled the tourist attractions and the places I was taken that were off the beaten path. I had crossed borders into other countries without my passport. I donned fatigues while smiling for the camera, and was sneaked into a foreign military base. I started to panic. What was happening to me? Why did I feel so out of control, and at the same time so controlled by others?

I was scared, exhausted and miserable by the time my mother dropped me off at the airport the next day. Her last words before I got out of her car were, "I moved across the world to get as far away from you as I could." I sat at the airport realizing that I was going back to Minnesota alone. I had no parents, no siblings that I was in contact with on a regular basis, and no extended family to call upon. There were no adults in my life. I felt incredibly lonely. I was going "home" to be alone.

In my two weeks overseas I had taken six rolls of film. When I went to pick up my pictures, only five rolls had been developed. The more I insisted that I had dropped off six rolls, the more the photo shop attendant insisted that it was only five. I know I had six rolls of film. I remember bringing them to the photo shop. In the two days I had been back, jetlagged and trying to sort out what happened during my trip, I found myself doubting and questioning everything. I pulled the car over and went through the pictures. Tucked inside one of the envelopes was a picture of me smiling tensely at the camera wearing Gabe's military cap.

Everything inside me shuddered. The very next day, I received a call to get back on a plane and return to the Middle East.

Chapter 12
QUAY

When I received the phone call to come back to the Middle East, I didn't give a thought to saying no. I was told I was a fearless butterfly who *surely* wanted to come back overseas. I was told where to pick up my plane ticket and where to withdraw $1,000 from a bank account to give to my roommate Grace. That amount of money would cover rent and the care and feeding of my cat for months. I told both Grace and my friend Mary that I had fallen in love with a boy overseas and I was going to stay with him for a while. Mary thought it was odd that after only knowing this boy for a short while I would pack up and leave, but I left no room for discussion.

I didn't give much thought to what I was leaving behind until I was settled in on the long flight. It was then that the reality of leaving behind my cat, Carlotta, struck me. She loved me unconditionally and I loved her. I felt disappointed in myself for leaving her behind without a second thought. Tears rolled down my face as I began thinking that I might never see her again, but I quickly wiped them away telling myself to forget about the cat, she was better off without me.

When I was back in my seat on the plane after a short layover, a couple approached me. The woman said, "Aren't you a cute little one?" and suggested I put on the dress she handed to me. Feeling like I was in a trance, I agreed, took the dress, and changed in the tiny bathroom.

The same woman was waiting for me when I took my seat. She gave me a hair brush and told me how pretty I looked. It hadn't occurred to me to ask this couple who they were or why they were giving me clothes. I was operating on no sleep, and a tangle of confusion about why I was going back to a country where the only person I knew didn't want to see me. In spite of this, I was calmed by how friendly and sweet the couple was, and I found myself feeling as pretty as they told me I looked.

After deplaning and going through customs, with my suitcase firmly in hand, I walked toward the glass partition and saw my mother, Arik, and his friend waiting for me. My stomach sank. As we drove away in my mother's car, no one spoke. I didn't have any idea where we were going. She stopped the car near a small, dusty town and told us that was as far as she was driving.

My mother hadn't even said hello when I arrived, but when she stopped the car, she looked at me and said, "Don't call me." As totally rejected and abandoned as I felt, I replied as snotty as I could, "Don't worry, I won't." She left me alone in the city of Quay with Arik and his friend. Arik took my suitcase, and he and his friend chatted casually to each other as we walked the few blocks to where I would be living the next three and a half weeks. I had no idea where we were or why. A surge of panic rose in my throat as I realized I had no way to leave and no one to turn to.

My mind exploded with what felt like little electric shocks as we walked through the paper-thin door into a tiny, two-room, hot and stuffy bungalow. There was a little kitchen with two folding metal chairs and no table. The only other room had a single bed and a wardrobe for clothes. There was a door and a small window covered by a darkened shade in the room with the bed, and a door off the kitchen. I had never seen such a small living space and wondered where the bathroom was. When I asked, Arik showed me a cement outhouse with a toilet, a little sink and a shower head. The bathroom was the worst shock to my American girl brain. Arik and his friend saw the look of horror on my face. He laughed, but his friend, who spoke a little bit of English, said, "It's okay."

That evening Arik invited some of his friends over and we sat outside. They were talking and laughing but I felt miserable and exhausted. I could tell that sometimes I was their topic by the way they looked at me during the conversation. The friend who came with us from the airport asked if he could practice speaking English with me. Of course, I said yes, thinking I was making a new friend. I saw him two other times: once when he stopped by to drop off a couple of elementary primer books so I could start to learn the language, and another time when Arik took me out on a Friday night to meet with the same group of people.

After everyone left, my fear of Arik and I living together in this bungalow fully set in. He told me that he would be going to his army base every day and that I would be staying here. Overwhelmed with sadness and homesickness, and reeling with exhaustion, I eventually fell asleep, but with my eyes on his gun leaning against the wall.

I spent my days in total isolation. I sat outside on the back steps in the scorching heat and stared. There was no radio or books, except for the primers written in a language I didn't understand. I had nothing to do but sit and stare at the outhouse in the backyard. I had been warned not to leave the house or walk around the town. A woman who lived on the other side of the bungalow would sometimes come out in the yard with her baby. There was a solid fence between the two yards but I could hear her talk to her child. I was desperate for someone to talk to, but I knew better than to reach out to her; even though I knew that she knew, I was there.

Arik would come home in the evening with fish or meat for one meal. We had no leftover food in the refrigerator and nothing in the cupboards. After dinner he would try to teach me the language from the primers. I was a terrible student. I just wanted to go home. I loved to read and I missed reading books or seeing anything printed in English. After a couple of weeks the isolation from everything I knew and recognized was taking hold, wearing on my psyche.

One day Arik brought me a pencil and some paper. I sat on the back steps and wrote a letter to my friend Mary. I knew it would never be mailed and I knew that anyone could read the letter, so I wrote only two lines. I wrote that I was living in a small town, the weather was hot and I drew a little picture. Arik took the letter from me, read it, and tossed it away.

Something I remembered from our lessons was that he told me that it was an insult to put your pointer finger up and wag it, like we do when we tell people to wait a moment in the U.S. I decided that was a good thing to tuck away. During our time together when my pain and frustration would get to a boiling point, I would wag my finger at him and relish in his shock. It was my only real defense against him and I enjoyed how he scowled with the insult. This was my small way of showing him that I wasn't afraid of him. He was often frustrated by the American things I did and I think my being defiant by wagging my finger threw him off balance. Those times although few and far between, left me feeling a little bit empowered. Those moments gave me a short reprieve from my breaking mind, heart, and soul.

Some weekends Arik and I walked to his father's nearby apartment. Although he was stand-offish and gruff when he met me, when he learned where my father was born and raised he softened a bit. The few times we visited him, he made us schnitzel and since I always felt starved, I ate with fervor. Every time I took a bite of food Arik would tell me I was fat. He would say it was amazing that even if he kept food from me, I was still fat. I knew that wasn't true, I weighed less than a hundred pounds, but every time he said it I felt like I should never put food in my mouth again. When he walked behind me as we climbed the steps to his father's apartment he would comment on how fat I was. One time we went to his sister's house for dinner. I couldn't understand a word they were saying until he told his sister I was fat. I have no idea what she said back to him.

Twice we went into downtown Quay. The first time was sundown on a Friday night when all the shops closed and everyone gathered in the street. We were going to meet Arik's friends. I remember I was wearing my watch and as we were walking down the street a man asked me what time it was. I had no idea what he had asked but he pointed to my watch. I let him see the time. Arik grabbed my arm and moved me quickly away. He told me not to talk to anyone I didn't know, which was everyone except him. After so much time alone, I enjoyed being in a crowd. It was exciting to be with a group of people my own age. They were laughing, having fun, and although I didn't understand most of what they were saying, being out amongst people gave me a boost. It eased the pain of my loneliness.

The second time we went into town was to buy food. Arik had come home with money and said we could get some food for the house. I absolutely hate milk. I can't drink it without gagging, but when I saw a little container of milk, it reminded me of home. We have milk in America, and I craved anything that reminded me of home. I picked up the container and brought it to the counter. The woman behind the counter shook her head twice pulling the milk carton away from me. She wouldn't let me buy anything in the store. Arik said it is because she knew I was an American and a stranger. I felt hurt and sad. I couldn't call my mother, I had no way to get home and I was painfully lonely, isolated, and confused. I couldn't understand why all this was happening to me, and why I couldn't buy a carton of milk.

Before we walked back home, Arik bought a chocolate bar. We shared it and even though he told me I was going to get fat from the candy, he shared it gleefully. It tasted like heaven to me. I could feel myself smile as I ate my piece of it, and for that moment I felt happy.

That night Arik told me the story partly in pantomime, of how he purposely shot himself in the stomach to get out of the army. He was very animated and showed me the bullet scar on his abdomen. I laughed at just how crazy and stupid he was to try to shoot himself with his own gun. Between the chocolate bar and Arik's dancing around in front of me like an idiot I think I had a sense of peace for a few moments.

I tried to shower when he was gone during the day. One day while showering, I felt a tingle go up my spine and the hair stand up on my neck. I turn around to find Arik staring at me with a look of hatred, power, and lust. His look was so dark and unnerving that I felt like he was going to hurt me. He told me that Americans were disgusting, because we use the same soap for all parts of our body instead of a different soap for our private parts. He said this as he pointed to my very naked body. I felt exposed, ugly, and disgusting. Shivering under the cold water and his cold stare, I realized just how much he hated me. I just wanted to go home. I still didn't know why I was being held prisoner. Arik wouldn't tell me why I was there, and there was no way I was going to disobey him by walking into town to find someone else to talk to.

The worst moment I had in Quay was the day that Arik angrily took me by the arm and shoved me out to the back yard next to the bathroom. There, all over the grass were pieces of toilet paper and used tampons. He was furious and called me all kinds of names. I didn't know that you couldn't flush tampons down the outside toilet. I had clogged the system and everything backed up into the yard. I was humiliated. He called me a stupid girl, a stupid, disgusting American. I felt my stomach roll over. I was red with shame as Arik continued to hurl insults, and I went back inside the house to curl up on the bed.

One day Arik finally announced that we were leaving. I had endured over three weeks of isolation, with him assaulting me, threatening me with his gun, and humiliating me. At the same time, I had formed a strange bond with him. We ate together, tried to teach one another our language, and sometimes had consensual sex. I depended on him. He came home to me every night. By the time we left there, he was the only person in my life I could count on.

We left my clothes in the small house and got on a bus. Arik was wearing his army fatigues with the ever-present gun hanging off his shoulder. As we were getting on the bus, an old lady pushed me aside and shoved ahead of me to board the bus first. That was my last memory of Quay: a bitchy old woman pushing me aside. I hated the people who lived in that town. They were rude, prejudiced against Americans, and didn't have indoor plumbing.

I felt invisible on the bus. Arik told me he was taking me to my mother's house. I hadn't spoken with her since she dropped us off on the edge of town. He deposited me with her and left. I felt rejected and abandoned as he walked away. What was I going to do without him? My mother served me some food and I went outside to eat in her garden rather than under her nasty glare.

Later, petting her two cats, I realized I had rarely thought of the cat that I had left behind. I was almost completely detached from my old life, but at the same time I was trying to detach from the hell-hole of isolation that I had shared with Arik for nearly four weeks.

Chapter 13
THE REASON I'M OVERSEAS

The day after I arrived at my mother's house she told me we are going for a drive. As we drove, she droned on about how she had moved out of the country to get away from me, and yet there I was again. I didn't respond. I sat silent, feeling the gnawing pain of knowing that I wasn't wanted by anyone, anywhere. As the miles slipped by, I kept wishing I could just evaporate and become the nothingness I felt that I was.

We pulled into a parking area off a dusty road. There, waiting for us, or more specifically waiting for me, was Daniel. I instantly went cold inside and felt my stomach roil with nausea. I hadn't seen him since the morning Arik and I came back from our overnight on the army base. I had completely forgotten about him, and thought I would never have to see him again.

My mother and I got out of the car and walked over to him. The two of them talked for a few minutes and then she turned around, got in the car and drove off. No goodbye, no see you later, no telling me where she was going or when she was coming back. My mother simply turned around, got in the car and left me. As I watched her drive away and looked over at Daniel, fear began snaking its way through my body.

There was a river just beyond the parking lot. I followed Daniel's lead as he walked toward it, through a park. It was a dusty, dirty area with a rocky edge bordering the narrow river, but there were a lot of people in the park and children playing along the river bank. The people around me seemed happy, chattering and laughing. I felt as if I were in a dream. I was standing in full view, but feeling invisible.

Daniel told me about how dangerous this area was. This was enemy territory and he called the river by name. I had heard of this ancient river in Sunday school and although I was scared, I was also intrigued. At the same time as I was terrified to be there alone with Daniel, I knew I would never have the chance to be in this historic spot again. I don't know how my mind had room for all that, but it did.

We stood watching the river for a while. The whole area was dirty and felt really poor. I knew we looked terribly out of place. Daniel said, "Come." I turned and walked behind him as he led the way into the dusty town.

I wasn't intrigued by the river any longer. With each step I become more anxious. Soon there was cold sweat dripping down my back, and my heart thumped loudly in my chest. As we walked into the little town, I noticed how dusty it was, how run down the houses were. I had never been in any place like this before. Daniel walked next to me with an air of confidence and power. I was afraid to be with him but also felt protected by his control.

Looking off to my left, I saw a young boy sitting on a flat roof top. He looked dirty, vacant or distant. Actually, I'm not sure what the expression on his face was. What I focused on was that he was holding a gun. It was the same kind of gun I had seen slung on the arms of the soldiers, but this was the first time I'd seen a child casually, confidently holding one. I looked away quickly, vowing to see only what was straight ahead. I no longer cared about anything but what was directly in front of me.

Daniel led me down one of the narrow streets and into a house. It appeared to be made of cement and was very plain, like all the other houses on the street. There wasn't anything that distinguished this house as different from any other house we passed; until we got inside. It was devoid of all things that would make it a home. There was no real furniture, no pictures on the walls, nothing that showed that anyone lived here. We walked through the front room and past a guard. In a fog, I followed Daniel down some stairs and into a tunnel. Not a basement, but a tunnel. This part of the world has recently become well known for its system of tunnels beneath borders, but back then I had never fathomed that something like this could exist.

The space was fairly wide, not narrow at all. There were lights recessed into the wall that were neither bright nor dim. There were large alcoves in my peripheral vision but I can't be sure if they led anywhere. I kept looking straight ahead, feeling as if I was in a dream. I didn't hear anyone talking until we came to a larger entrance. I saw a table with papers spread out on it. A huge man in a military uniform was talking to a group of soldiers standing around the table. He had a weapon on his belt, but what struck me the most about him was that he looked more confident than any other person I had ever seen in my life. He commanded attention when he spoke. Daniel approached him and they began conversing.

The man turned, glanced in my direction, and gestured for me to come closer to the table. He showed me two pictures of someone who looked vaguely familiar. One of the pictures was the man getting out of his car, the other picture was a full-on head shot of the same person. He told me I was going to go through a tunnel like this one to a neighboring country and meet up with the man in the picture. He told me I was to have a date with him. It slowly began to dawn on me who the man in the picture was, and exactly what they were asking me to do. Standing there looking down at the picture, I began to shake my head and heard myself say, "No, No." I didn't say it loud or with any force. I just stood there shaking my head saying, "No."

The huge man in the uniform quickly rounded and smacked me hard across the face. I didn't see it coming. I stood there in shock, my hand on my stinging cheek, looking at the ground.

Daniel took a few steps toward me, stopping inches in front of my face, and in a calm but firm tone said, "You belong to us, this is now your life." He continued, "You are going to die with us. You can make that come sooner or later, but I assure you, that you will do what we ask."

Daniel turned and spoke with the other man for a few minutes in their language, then with a nod and in plain English, I heard the directive, "Go back and get her ready." I was escorted out of the tunnel and into a waiting car.

As the car slowly drove away I stared straight ahead. I didn't look back and I didn't look around the neighborhood. I was ringing with shock. First, I was still trying to comprehend that I had been in a tunnel, and questioning whether or not what they had asked me to do was real. Second, I was trying to comprehend that these people truly did have control over my life and were going to kill me. I had no context for any of this, but I had no reason to doubt the seriousness of their intent. I coped the best way I could, by dissociating. I didn't have much time at all to forget what had just happened to me, because we were quickly at our destination. The driver dropped me off in the same parking area by the river, where my mother sat in her car waiting for me.

When I saw her, disbelief and anger welled up from the depths of my soul. This was a horrible replay of the times she had dropped me off to be a victim of any number of rituals and sexual perversions. She was prostituting me out once again, but this time under the guise of her country's best interest.

I was too angry and hurt to speak a word to her as I got in the car and slammed the door. We drove silently back to her house. I could feel the hot sting of tears roll down my cheeks. I let them fall, but kept my face hidden from her. I knew if she saw me crying, that she would turn the whole situation back on herself with another tirade of how much I constantly inconvenienced her.

The next day Arik suddenly walked into my mother's house. I was stunned to see him. I didn't know if I would ever see him again once I left Quay. I formed a strong trauma bond with him. Even though he had done some terrible things to me, I was comforted with thinking I was reasonably sure he wouldn't kill me. That is how broken my thinking had become. I was quickly figuring out there were two groups of people in my life: those who would kill me and those who would not.

Arik and I walked across the street to the beach and sat down in the sand to watch the waves and the sunset. He drew a big heart in the sand and I put our initials in it. How strange and surreal that innocent act was. I was a young girl pretending I was with a boy who liked me, and he was a young boy pretending to be with a girl who liked him.

Neither one of us wanted to leave the beach for the house. I asked him where my clothes were. He told me they were still at the house in Quay and that his sister had gone through them and tried some on. The familiar anger I often had toward him swelled in my belly, but I tamped it down and told myself to keep watching the waves.

Arik told me we were going to go to the city the next day. I saw he was nervous, but watching him, I could tell he had a harder edge about him than I had seen before. I didn't pretend to know what was going through his mind. Our language barrier was often insurmountable, but had I guessed what he was thinking, it would have been that things were moving way beyond his control and he was afraid, too.

When we got back to the house, Ron was lying on the couch reading a magazine and my mother was cleaning the kitchen. Arik and I sat silently in the living room until it was time to go to bed. The next morning we were dropped off at the bus station to ride to the city.

Arriving in the busy, large and noisy city, we threaded our way down several narrow and winding streets until we came to a non-descript looking apartment building. All the dilapidated buildings and doors looked the same. If I had become separated from Arik, I would never have found my way back to this building.

We climbed the stairs to the apartment and once inside, I headed straight for the shower. My mother had given me a bag with clothes and after I got cleaned up I put on an orange gauzy flowing skirt and white shirt. I felt clean, fresh, and beautiful.

We grabbed my purse that only held three items: my brush, my passport, and $50 I had brought from home. We headed into the city to go to a movie. For a moment I pretended I was a happy tourist going out for a night on the town. I let myself feel the same way with Arik that I felt on the beach: a boy and girl on a date. After the movie, I watched other people strolling along, carefree and laughing. I noticed a cute couple holding hands, talking sweetly to each other as they walked down the street.

I yearned for Arik to hold my hand and talk sweetly to me. He didn't hold my hand. He walked next to me with tense body language. Any fantasy I had of putting behind the last month flew out of my mind, replaced with the knowledge that I would never have that. I would never have a boy hold my hand and talk sweetly to me.

I couldn't forget the last thirty-six hours. After being held in isolation for nearly a month, my mother had taken me to a rendezvous with a powerful and dangerous man. I had been ordered to have sex with a high-profile dignitary of a foreign country, and told he would just be one of many men I would be set up with, for the rest of my life.

I didn't know how long or short my life was going to be, but I felt like a walking dead girl. Arik and I slowly made our way back to the apartment. Climbing the stairs, feeling exhausted, I had no idea that the following morning would begin ten days of the most horrific terror I could imagine.

Chapter 14
DAY TWO

I never got used to the silence between Arik and me. Our language barrier was so great that small talk was impossible. Little things like reviewing the movie we saw, or talking about the people we had seen walking along the street was out of the question. The silence kept me thinking. All I thought about was what might happen to me next. These were really just empty thoughts, because I had absolutely no idea what would come next and no context to try to anticipate my fate.

When we got back to the apartment I put my purse on the window ledge. Looking out the window I was struck by how ugly this part of the city was. Everything was dark and gray. The buildings looked industrial and as dilapidated as the apartment we were in.

Soon after we settled in for the evening there was a knock at the door. A man came in carrying a green satchel and began talking with Arik. I sat on the worn sagging couch while they talked by the door. I didn't understand a word they were saying. After the man left, Arik put the satchel on the chair and started to tell me with shreds of English and a lot of gesturing that I was going to carry the satchel tomorrow.

He was anxious, trying very hard to communicate and make me understand that what he was asking of me was important. I wasn't having any part of it and got up to go to the bathroom. I felt the same as I did in the tunnel when they showed me pictures and told me what I was to do. I didn't want to carry someone else's ugly satchel or anything that wasn't mine. As I came out of the bathroom and Arik began repeating to me what I had to do the next morning, I angrily blurted, "Fuck you." There is no language barrier with that particular expression. Furious, Arik crossed the room in a flash and had me by the throat against the wall. He yelled, "You are a stupid girl. You must obey. Do you want to get us killed?"

Looking into his eyes as Arik choked me, I felt a kind of fear I had never felt before. His face was contorted with anger. Just as suddenly, getting control of his emotions, he let go of my throat and walked off into the bedroom. I slid down the wall and sat on the floor. My neck and throat felt crushed. I was panting in fear, and trying to force air back into my lungs.

I don't know how much time passed before I got up to go to bed. Surprisingly, I crawled into bed next to Arik. I was terrified and I didn't want to be alone. Even if Arik killed me, at least I wouldn't be alone. This is the same boy that the day before on the beach, I was convinced I was safe with because he would only assault me, not kill me. Now I wasn't so sure. But he was still the safest person in the world to me at that point.

The next morning I dressed in shorts, a t-shirt, and leather sandals. He puts on his army pants and white t-shirt and made a show of grabbing the gun he always carried slung over his shoulder. I was quiet as he handed me the satchel. It felt light and I had no idea what, if anything was inside, but I grabbed it and nodded that I was ready to go. We left the apartment and walked to the open-air bus terminal. There were so many buses; I remember thinking, "How could a person figure out which bus to take in this maze?" As we neared a little boulevard I noticed how beautiful and blue the sky was. Arik had positioned me on his right side, the side of his gun. I was petrified of his gun and he knew it. Still feeling numb from the night before, I obediently walked beside him, willing to do anything he told me to do.

As we crossed the boulevard the whole scene was rocked by a tremendously loud noise. There was breaking glass, screaming, and chaos. Falling down hard on my hands and knees, I screamed and held my ears. Arik pulled me up, yelling at me. I blindly grabbed his hand and started running with him breathless and terrified, leaving the satchel behind. My adrenalin was pumping, pushing me forward, faster and faster.

We finally stopped a few blocks away and caught our breath. My mind couldn't make sense of what had just happened. I was dazed. I had no idea a bomb had just exploded next to us. I had never seen or heard a bomb before. I had no reason to think the sound that I heard was a bomb. I had no point of reference for any of this. I did know, deep inside, that something really terrible had just happened, and it was dawning on me that this might be the life I had been assigned to, just a few days before in the tunnel.

Arik found his way to his friend's apartment building and pushed the button at the bottom of the stairs to turn the hall lights on. We climbed three sets of cement steps. My knees were screaming in pain. A boy about our age opened the door. The whites of his eyes were yellow. He saw the odd way I looked at him and told me in beautiful English that he had jaundice. He looked terribly sick. We followed him into another room where he sat down exhausted. There were books on his shelf and I remember feeling relief when I saw them. As upset and confused as I was, I was comforted by reading their English titles, as Arik and the boy spoke quietly with one another.

Arik suddenly told me to take off my shoes. He stuffed them under his arm and grabbed my hand with an urgent look in his eyes. I heard footsteps and muffled sounds coming down the hall behind the room we were in. Before I had time to think the door bust open and Arik yelled, "Run!" We ran out of the apartment and down the cement steps. I ran, bare-footed and panicky. I didn't know what was going on; I was just trying to keep up with Arik.

Finally, at a low cement wall, Arik stopped, leaning against it to try to catch his breath. I leaned over it and threw up. I hadn't eaten anything since we left my mother's house, but fear drove what little was inside of me hurling over the wall. I was dirty, terrified, and gasping for air. Arik was clearly afraid too, struggling to pull himself together. After several minutes, he caught his breath and calmly said, "Come."

I don't know for certain what happened in that apartment or to the boy with the yellow eyes, but I was beginning to piece together that this was all part of a plan to get me ready for something; to scare me into submission.

We found our way back to our apartment in silence. We showered, and Arik gave me clean clothes as he packed a backpack and sleeping bags. He changed out of his fatigues, but packed them. He changed into short shorts and an ugly orange shirt. I remember thinking how funny his outfit looked with his army boots.

We left the apartment and walked in the opposite direction than we had earlier. We were exhausted, scared and silent. My knees ached, my body hurt, and my mind felt broken but numb. I tried not to make sense of what happened earlier, but felt like throwing up every time it crept into my consciousness. We eventually came to a bus stop. Arik bought sandwiches and pop and we boarded the bus. I never thought to ask where we were going. It didn't matter to me in the least.

Leaning against the bus window, I couldn't believe that not long ago, I was living with my cat Carlotta and a roommate Grace and had a best friend named Mary. Part of me thought they too, blew up that morning. It was easier to think that my life before the tunnel was gone; erased. If everyone was dead, I wouldn't have to think about missing them, or face that I was never going home again.

I felt myself trying to separate from the humanity I saw every day. The people, sitting next to me on the bus or walking past me on the street, looked normal. I saw the sparkle in their eyes, their easy laughter and smiles. I was the only one with fear twisting in my diaphragm. I tried hard to dissociate from my life. I couldn't begin to deal with the trauma of what had happened, and what might still be expected of me. I felt nothing but terror. I was a walking dead girl.

Chapter 15
THE SIDE TRIP

As soon as we got on the bus, Arik told me he wanted to make sure I talked so everyone would know that he was with an American girl. I was exhausted, upset and in no mood to talk to anyone, so I didn't. My only defiance in the last 24 hours was to stay as quiet as I could. Blending in, I was just another local taking the bus.

Arik started talking with a girl sitting across the aisle and I found myself watching him. He was so easy with his speech in his own language. I wondered for a moment if he was flirting with this girl. She didn't seem to notice that I was with him. I could feel myself shut down with each passing mile. I kept my eyes averted and didn't say a word. My stomach churned as I realized that I might never hear my own language again. I didn't notice the landscape change because I wasn't really looking out the window, but staring into space. I felt as if I was taking a ride to nowhere. I was nobody going nowhere.

The bus dropped us off in the desert, in the heat of the day. Arik grabbed the backpack and we walked along the side of the road. We hadn't talked to each other in hours, so I didn't know where we were or where he intended to take us. He pointed to a rocky hill off to the right and said, "Climb." I didn't want to climb. I was worried because I was only wearing sandals and not hiking boots. I was afraid he might even push me off the cliff.

Seeing my hesitation, Arik insisted, trying to tell me that there were animals for us to see up there. So we climbed. I was so afraid. I had no idea where to put my hands or feet, but Arik kept looking back at me and repeating, "Come." His demeanor was

94

light-hearted and encouraging, so I kept climbing. Between the fear of falling off the rocks, and having no idea where I was going, I was proud of myself. I had never done anything like this before and I found myself enjoying the adventure.

When we reached the top of the hill we could see several small goats grazing off in the distance. Arik told me they were ibex. We sat down and watched them and took in the scenery below us. For a few moments we were just two people on vacation. I even felt myself smile as I sat there, safe on a high rocky hill with the sea in the distance and the desert all around us. We both let down our guard and relaxed for a little while. I let myself be just a girl on an adventure in a foreign land with a cute boy.

We climbed back down the rock face and headed across the road toward the sea. We played, splashing one another in the salt water. We laughed as we tried to keep our balance and used each other to float easily along the surface of the water. It felt strange to laugh. I hadn't made the sound of laughter for months. It felt as if someone else was there having fun in the sea, not me.

By the time we were out of the water, showered and dressed, it was late in the afternoon, close to evening. Arik said we were going to sleep in the park, on the beach. I was hungry and thirsty. He gave me water but said we had no food. I knew we had $50 in my purse, but he shook his head "no" when I asked if we could buy something. He pulled out some dried food and began eating it but wouldn't share. There were a few times when we were at the house in Quay that Arik hadn't shared his food with me. When he denied me food that evening, any illusion of an adventure with a cute boy quickly ended. I knew nothing had changed.

He laid out the sleeping bags and I got into mine without saying a word. I was tired and hungry, and the shock of the previous days had started to creep back into my head. Turning away from Arik, I fell asleep hating him. But the truth was that I didn't hate him. I was still dependent on him. He held my money, my water, my food, and my life in his hands. I convinced myself he was just a stupid boy, but I also knew I needed him.

We woke up early the next morning, cleaned up in the park bathrooms, and hiked along the desert road. It was a beautiful sandy, but stark landscape. Never in my wildest dreams did I think I'd be walking along in a desert. There was a beautiful, other-worldly feel to it. As we walked, Arik told me he was taking me to an ancient fortress built by a king. I had heard about this place from my father. It was a well known story and a huge tourist destination.

When we arrived I was awestruck; first by the sheer size of it and second by the historical significance and age of the structure. It was mind-boggling. Traveling the Middle East, the history of this area had never been lost on me. When my mind wasn't shutting down in fear, I would let myself think about whose footsteps I was walking in, thousands of years later. A sense of reverence sometimes washed over me.

There were a lot of Americans milling around and I was soothed by the sound of their English. Funny, the day before I had thought I'd never hear English spoken without a Middle Eastern or European accent again, and here I was immersed in the sound of my own language. I knew better than to reach out to any of the tourists, and so I kept my head down and enjoyed the ruins. I noticed that Arik was getting agitated and I didn't know why. Maybe he was thirsty and hungry like I was, or maybe this was the beginning of another bad day. I had no idea.

I found a bench and sat down surrounded by unearthed frescos from the ancient Roman times. I was fascinated. I could have sat there all day. The air was hot, we were baking in the sun, and the site was alive with language, alive with history. Arik and I looked over the high walls at the desert below. A strong, hot wind was blowing on my face and through my hair. It blew in from every direction and kept going. There were no trees to block it or muffle the sound. I had never felt or heard anything like this hot, dusty, unrelenting wind.

I felt Arik's mood change as we stood there. His body tensed up, and his mouth set itself in an angry scowl. He looked at me and said, "I'm going to leave you here." His words oozed hatred. I instinctively reacted just as I had in the tunnel, pleading, "No, No!" I wondered if this was how they were going to kill me. I imagined frying all alone in the desert, pounded by the hot wind.

In my peripheral vision I saw a man walking towards us. I turned to look at him because I sensed his very purposeful approach. I had never seen a man who carried himself like this before. He was tall, tanned, and well-groomed. He wore a short-sleeved shirt and neutral pants. I couldn't tell you his eye or hair color, or anything that stood out about his features, but he had the look of someone who could either kill you or save you in a moment. He exuded confidence. He wasn't afraid of anyone or anything.

As the man approached, he asked me if everything was okay. I stood still as a statue and didn't respond. He started talking to Arik, and I watched Arik's demeanor shrink. The man turned to me and put his hand on my arm. Before walking away, he said, "You will be okay. You are a fearless butterfly." I shivered at the name I'd been called as a child in the facility.

Fear and confusion had me plunging into the past. I felt in a trance as I nodded my head to acknowledge this man's comforting words. I knew that Arik wouldn't leave me in the desert now, but I also realized that we were being watched. Maybe that was what was making Arik so tense. Maybe his threat to leave me in the desert was his way of fighting for control of his own life, trying to escape the situation he was trapped in, too. He was silent as we descended from the top of the monument and sat at a dusty windswept bus stop, ready to make our way to the next destination.

I was afraid thinking about what had happened at those ruins. Neither one of us was in the mood to talk so I didn't bother to ask where we were going. I was past the point of feeling hungry, but I was desperately thirsty. It felt like my tongue was swelling. I was filthy from all the wind and dust, and ached for a shower. I looked out the bus window sullenly, knowing I had to put the last few days out of my mind.

We got to our destination late in the afternoon. Arik pointed to a boat launch and explained that we were going to take the ferry to an island. I had no interest in going on a boat. I was sick from hunger and thirst and nauseous from all the bus travel in the last 24 hours. The thought of getting on a ferry and riding the waves made my stomach churn. Miserable, I walked toward the ferry praying that I wouldn't throw up in front of all these strangers.

It was only a short boat ride to the island. It was hot and the air felt salty. The sun was high, blazing off the white sand. I followed Arik away from the tourist area to the other side of the small island. I sat near the water while he found shade beneath a cliff wall. He finally came over to sit next to me, saying that we had missed the last ferry and would have to sleep on the island that night. He stood up and walked away as my head pounded with panic. For the second time in a matter of hours, I had the very real fear that I was going to die alone in the desert.

Arik laid out the sleeping bags and I sat beside him. He was quiet and seemed smug. I hadn't eaten anything in over 24 hours and had very little water. I was feeling dizzy and sick from the sun and hot wind. I lay down and curled up in a ball waiting to die. Arik slept silently next to me.

Early the next morning the ferry dropped off the first round of happy tourists, ready to explore the island. We took the ferry back to the mainland and walked to the nearest bus station. I felt terribly sick. I was dizzy and fuzzy-headed, and my stomach was aching.

At the bus station Arik gave me my toothbrush and a change of clothes. As I headed for the bathroom, sickness started exploding out of me in waves. I had never been so violently ill in my life and was terrified. Hearing me, Arik came into the bathroom. He helped me wash up and then rushed out to buy me a can of grape soda.

He helped me onto the bus and was kind, letting me rest my head on his shoulder, but my nausea erupted with each bump. Every time the bus stopped to pick up or drop anyone off, I ran to the bathroom. At every stop, Arik bought me another can of grape soda. A few hours into our ride and with my head on his shoulder, I finally fell asleep. I'm sure he was afraid when he saw how sick I was. By now he knew that if something happened to me, he would be in deep trouble. I didn't care why he was being kind; I just wanted someone to be there with me. Hours later, we arrived at the town closest to my mother's house. From there we hitched a ride to her enclave and walked the final mile to her house. I didn't ask why we were going to my mother's house. I was just desperate to stop moving.

As soon as we got there, I was sick all over again. My mother said that I was severely dehydrated. I lay on her bathroom floor feeling floaty and ill, disconnected from my body. I felt like I was a nobody with *no* body. Later that same night my mother hosted a dinner party for Ron and the many men who were my father's friends. I lay on the bathroom floor for most of the night, listening as they talked, ate, and laughed.

I was desolate. My mother had once again, taken no care of me at all. Abandoned and miserable, I eventually found my way to the bedroom and slept. There was a glass of water on the nightstand and I took a few sips, fighting to keep it down. I was still sick the next morning when I woke up, but kept sipping the water and tried to eat. To this day, I remember the horror of being dehydrated.

When I saw Arik the next morning I found myself telling him how grateful I was for the soda he had bought for me. I should have been furious with him. He'd withheld food and water from me for more than 24 hours in the desert. Instead, I had a sickening trauma bond with him that left me appreciating the soda. That's how broken my mind and body had become in just five days since the tunnel.

Chapter 16
THE FARM

Later the next morning my mother, Arik, and I drove to the communal farm where Ron lived. I still wasn't feeling very well and was on guard seeing Arik's reaction when he found out where we were going. I thought he might be judgmental about this different way of living, but it may have been that he was nervous to be going into Ron's territory.

I didn't know what to expect. I had heard of communes but had a vision of tie-dyed hippies planting gardens, laughing, and singing. I should have known better. Ron was nothing like a hippie.

The farm was a very strange place. I felt like I had landed on another planet. Everyone lived in tiny barracks-like housing with the children living in separate quarters. This was incredibly foreign to me. We went to the cafeteria for dinner. Still feeling sick, I managed to only eat a few bites. I played with the food on my plate, but then stood up to throw it away. I had no idea that wasting food would cause such a stir. As I scraped my plate I heard a lot of tongue-clucking from the people around me. I didn't care. I was moody and sullen. Their opinion meant nothing to me because I knew they weren't going to threaten, choke, rape, or starve me. I knew I was safe because they weren't treating me as if I was invisible. They could see me, and they were reacting to my American-girl way of wasting food. Feeling the disapproval all around, I thought, God, is there anywhere in this country I can fit in?

After dinner, we walked to Ron's bungalow where his wife, daughter, and granddaughter were serving dessert. I was hugely uncomfortable sitting there, knowing that my mother was Ron's mistress. His wife had to have known about the affair, yet welcomed my mother into her house. His family accepted her without a problem.

Nearly every day of my life, my mother had told me she hated me. She told me she had moved to get away from me. She told me not to call her when she dropped me off in Quay, and ignored me as I lay sick on her bathroom floor. But in Ron's house she was flitting around, playing lovingly with his granddaughter and talking as if it was perfectly normal to be a part of their family. I despised her treatment of me, and felt sharply rejected as I watched her take gentle care of someone else's children.

Arik and I sat on the couch after dessert. Ron was in a chair by the door. I wanted to be anywhere but in that house, and Arik was growing more agitated by the minute.

As night fell we heard noises. There was consistent, loud banging. I startled and looked anxiously towards the door. Ron looked back at me amused and said, "That is us shooting at them. Not them shooting at us." No one else in the house seemed upset that gunfire was erupting within earshot, except Arik. His tension and fear matched mine.

The smirk on Ron's face as he spoke reminded me that I was still in the nightmare that was now my life. I felt trapped, with my stomach twisting. Arik and I sat on the couch like statues listening to the gunfire. Suddenly Ron said, "Okay, It's time to go now." We must not have moved fast enough for him, because his demeanor turned very stern. Arik saw it too, stood up, and grabbed my hand to pull me up.

A jeep was waiting outside. Arik and I got in. No one said goodbye as the driver pulled away from the house. I felt sick and sad knowing my mother was in the house with her new family and didn't care that I was leaving with yet another stranger. I sat in the back seat holding back tears, willing myself to think about nothing.

I felt the bumps in the road, but I was working hard to dissociate from what was happening. I didn't know if the driver was taking me to another tunnel, or to another country. Maybe this time I was being taken to die. I sat silently, going along for the ride.

Chapter 17
ONE TERRIBLE NIGHT

I sensed the jeep was taking us further north. It was starting to get dark. In the glow of twilight I could see the outline of trees as we slowed down. The jeep stopped on a dirt road at the edge of the woods. A soldier came to meet us and opened the door. He was dressed all in black. I had a hard time making out his features, but I had no problem identifying the gun he carried in his hands, or another strapped around his leg. He opened the door and without speaking, grabbed my arm and led me quickly into the woods.

Moving swiftly alongside the soldier, I realized I was hearing the same popping sounds that I'd heard at Ron's house, except they sounded louder and closer. Terror doesn't begin to explain what I was feeling as my heart began pounding. Why was I here? What was I supposed to do? I heard whizzing sounds and thought I saw bits of bark flying off the trees. Everything was happening so fast. Sounds of the shooting were echoing in my ears and through my body. We stopped and I cowered on the ground behind a tree, my legs bent tightly against my body, my hands covered my ears. I knew that the soldier who had led me out of the jeep was next to me and was shooting. In my head, the mantra, "It's us shooting at them, not them shooting at us," played over and over again.

Was this another part of getting me ready for my new life? Trying to stop my mind from spinning, I remembered that Daniel told me in the tunnel that what they were asking me to do was for the good of the country. How could shooting at people be good for the country?

When the shooting stopped, the soldier held out his hand and helped me stand up. Dazed and on wobbly legs, I staggered after him. Everything seemed to go into slow motion as he led me further into the woods. My nose burned with the smell of gun powder. The air felt cool and damp and the trees were outlined in black. I saw several fallen black trees; at least that's what I kept telling myself. What I couldn't allow myself to face, was that the fallen trees were actually wounded men.

I refused to let my mind truly comprehend what I was seeing, smelling, and hearing. With each slow-motion step, I convinced myself that what I was hearing was the late summer sound of cicadas. We passed a couple of soldiers standing around smoking. They didn't seem to notice me. They were relaxed. Why didn't they respond to a young girl walking through the woods in shorts and a tank top? They seemed unconcerned, as if I was supposed to be there.

As we moved past the carnage, I glanced back to my left and the scene hadn't changed. I began to realize that I had just experienced combat for the first time. If the point of this exercise was to desensitize me to the sound of guns, the smell of the dank woods, and the faces of wounded men, then I had failed the training. I was shaking, cold, and more petrified with every step. Tears stung my eyes and I told myself that I hated this fucking foreign country.

We had made it back to the jeep when I noticed the eerie quiet. I told myself that it was okay to leave now because the cicadas had gone back to sleep. Seeing Arik sitting quietly in the front seat of the jeep it occurred to me that I hadn't seen him in the woods. I never thought to ask him where he had been. I knew that I was never going to talk about what just happened. I sat in the back seat holding down my vomit as the jeep began rumbling along a dirt road. For a moment I entertained the thought we were driving back to Ron's and eventually, to my mother's house. That seemed to be the emerging pattern.

But it didn't take long to realize we weren't heading back to the farm or my mother's house. The road turned and we drove parallel to a fence. No one spoke. Arik looked straight ahead while I worked to keep myself from throwing up, my stomach lurching with each bump of the road. I felt like I was barely inside my body.

Suddenly, the jeep stopped. The driver got out and told us to stay in the vehicle as he walked away. Arik pointed to the fence and told me what country we were bordering. Feeling my panic swell and without thinking, I opened the door and blindly started running in the opposite direction of the fence. It was a crazy, arm-flapping run for my life that I had tried a few times in the past.

I didn't stop to think how angry the soldier would be that I took off, I just knew I had to get away. Before I got very far, Arik had overtaken me and pulled me to the ground. He wrapped his forearm around my neck. Angrily hissing in my ear, he began calling me, "Stupid, stupid girl." Feeling his forearm around my neck, I went slack with exhaustion and utter hopelessness. He pulled me back to the jeep and I sat down, completely spent. My arms and legs felt like they were made of lead and my skin felt thick.

The soldier who was driving the jeep came back through the fence with a man. The man climbed in the back next to me and I noticed the mood had changed. I thought they were angry at me for running, but soon realized that the new tone had nothing to do with me.

The man we had picked up was quiet and seemed introspective. He wore the same green military pants I saw everyone wear, along with a dark t-shirt and black high top military boots. I could smell fear emanating from him. I knew

106

that scent from smelling it on myself. He was sweating, his jaw was set and clenched, and he wore a look of resignation.

The terrain changed as we drove away from the fence. It became weedy, rough, and barren. It seemed as if we were literally driving into the middle of nowhere. We got to a cement building that looked like a house with a flat roof. There was a tower or some sort of tall structure next to it, but nothing else around but barren land. We got out of the jeep and walked into the building. I stood in the main room while Arik, the driver, and the man went into another one. No one said anything to me about joining them, so I just stood by the door and waited. Three soldiers stood in the corner. I didn't know what to do with my hands, and I suddenly felt very small, dirty, and ugly.

The three soldiers stopped talking and I could feel their eyes running over my body. Even though I kept my own eyes lowered, I felt humiliated standing there being sized up like their next meal. I sat down in the corner against the wall thinking that I would rather die than live this life that had been laid out for me. I felt absolutely alone and just wanted a way to stop the insanity that had become my existence.

I heard movement behind me. A huge, powerful-looking man came into the room. Behind him, the man from the jeep was brought in and put into a chair by the wall. He was sweating profusely. His shirt was soaked with perspiration and he seemed hurt. He slumped in the chair. The powerful man gruffly ordered me to stand up. I quickly obeyed. As I stood up, he handed me a knife. He pointed to the man in the chair and said, "Kill him." He pushed me towards the man and I landed on him; my hand bracing my fall against his stomach. I was struck dumb with fear and panic. The people in the tunnel had been telling me the truth. I was either going to do what they told me, or I was going to die.

I went as feral as a trapped animal. I dropped the knife, and started screaming, flapping my hands with frenetic energy. In a panic I ran to the wall, slid down it, and began to bang my head as hard as I could against it. I knew I'd rather die than kill someone. I hit my head harder and harder, telling myself to die, die, die, over and over again.

I heard my head banging against the wall, but I also heard yelling and orders being barked. The powerful man was enraged and screamed, "Do what I told you!" There was so much noise and commotion that I didn't know what was real from what was scrambling in my brain.

The man pulled me off the floor into a standing position, yelling at me the entire time. I saw that the man in the chair was slumped over with a mark on his forehead. I was completely terrified and certain I was going to die. I had a vague sensation of something wet on my face and mouth and felt myself lose control of my bladder as I collapsed to the floor. I held my breath, feeling that I might never breathe again.

I felt myself being dragged from the room. I was still holding my breath. The only sound I heard now was the pounding of my heart. Before I could process what was happening, I was dropped into a shower. I felt the water run down my head and body and crouched on the dirty cement shower floor. I felt myself being stripped naked, but all I could focus on was the dirt and smell washing down the drain. I could feel myself shutting down as my broken mind tried to block out everything.

Someone pulled me out of the shower and led me to a back room where there was a bed. It must have been very late in the night by now. Arik was lying there looking scared and ragged. I climbed in next to him but turned away, lying on my side. He whispered in perfect English with as much venom as he could muster, "You will be a killer *and* a whore."

I absorbed his words deep into my psyche as I fell asleep. I was totally exhausted. My skull hurt from banging my head against the wall and my right arm hurt from being pulled into the bathroom like a rag doll. Just 24 hours earlier I was recovering from serious dehydration. That whole day, from the moment we set foot on the farm until I was lying in this bed, had been nothing but abject terror, confusion, and pain.

An eerie calm came over me as I drifted off to sleep. I felt the sting of shame from peeing on the floor. I felt dirty from the three soldiers leering at me as if I was a piece of meat. I felt old because my adolescent naivety had been cruelly torn away without explanation. I felt I would never be worthy of love. Who could love a killer and a whore? Despite all these feelings I was somehow still calm. There was nothing else to do at that moment but drift off into sleep.

The next morning the powerful man from the night before, came into the bedroom with a new t-shirt and shorts. I felt an old anger rise in me. Here I was again, being given clothes that weren't mine and that I would never have picked out for myself to wear. My indignation blew away quickly though, as the man cupped his right hand on the left side of my face and said, "We are very disappointed in you, but not to worry, we will find something to do with you." I knew he was lying to me. I remember what Daniel had said to me in the tunnel. Obviously, I had failed at every task they had given me. I knew the moment that his big, warm, rough hand touched my cheek that I was going to die.

He ordered me to get dressed because it was time to go. I dressed quickly and followed Arik out of the room. I realized we were walking through the same room that was the scene of the carnage the night before. My stomach roiled with nausea. My peripheral vision caught the dark stains on the floor and the knocked-over chair. The smells filled my nostrils. On the verge of throwing up, I couldn't pretend that this was all just a bad dream.

We walked outside and there was a helicopter waiting for us. I was terrified. I thought they were going to take me up in the air and throw me out. I would tumble to my death. I started to take two steps backwards when I saw that one of the people in the front seat was Ron. He was looking at me with disgust. I was so confused. How did he know where I was? Could he have known all along where I was going, and what was going to happen that night? Could he really put me in that kind of danger? Whoever was behind me pushed my back to start my motion forward. Arik and I climbed aboard and we took off.

We landed somewhere a short distance away, and waiting there for us, was my mother. Ron, Arik, and I got into her car and we drove to a park filled with people. She put out a picnic lunch. I sat there in shock. Could this be happening? How could we be having a picnic in a park after what happened the night before? My mother and Ron chatted away, but Arik and I ate silently.

Leaning over, Arik picked a red flower from the garden alongside us and gave it to me. I put it in my hair, walked over to Arik and sat on his lap. I so wanted to be a normal girl with a pretty flower from a boy who liked her. I think Arik wanted the same thing. As much as he called me names and abused me, just a few months before he had been a young naive boy from a small town. He held me on his lap with his arms tightly around me, and we sat that way for a few minutes. I could feel an intense hatred building in me for Ron, a hatred that I would carry with me until the day I heard of his death.

When our picnic was finished and they were packing up, Ron started railing against me about what was expected of me, and how I had let them all down. I flew into a rage and began yelling. I stomped up and down yelling, "You are *not* my father, so stop trying to act like it." I don't know why that came pouring out of my mouth, but I immediately felt deflated. I felt ridiculous and small. I could feel the weight of the red flower. I whipped it out of my hair, threw it on the ground and stamped on it until it was shredded, ground it into the blacktop. I made my way to my mother's car.

We were all silent on the long drive back. Instead of taking us to her house, my mother dropped Arik and I off at the bus station. We took a bus back to the apartment in the city. As much as I had hated being there a few days ago, it suddenly felt like home. Ignoring the wall where Arik had held me by the throat, I took a shower, left my clothes on the bathroom floor in a heap and went to bed. Arik came into the bedroom with my clothes, telling me how disgusting I was. I felt my face redden with embarrassment, but at least the Arik I had grown to equally like and hate, was back, and feeling confident. I would rather be around the confident Arik who was in control than the one that was frightened and fidgety.

The next morning, he told me we were going to a beach town in the south of the country. I didn't respond. I didn't care where we were going. I would have followed him anywhere and not asked why. I knew by now that wherever I went, it would only be for a short time, it wouldn't be safe, and that no one could be trusted. I was relieved when he donned his familiar backpack and handed me my purse with $50 in it. Somehow carrying my own purse out of that apartment made the world a sane place for one short moment.

We stopped at the market and bought sandwiches and soda, and we boarded the bus headed south. This time, Arik didn't ask me to talk on the bus and he wasn't flirting with other passengers. We were both silent, staring into the nothingness. My stomach was in a tight knot. My mind would spin out of control if I replayed the events of the day before. So instead, I thought of my cat Carlotta. Would I ever see her again? And if I did would she remember me?

Chapter 18
DAY NINE

We arrived in a beautiful resort town in the early afternoon. I hadn't seen any place like this in the country so far. It felt exotic and was bustling with tourists. There were a lot of shops, smiling people and a beautiful beach. I didn't know what sea this was but it looked stunning. It felt strange to be surrounded by so many vacationing people. How could they be so happy and carefree? My brain couldn't compute how oblivious people were. The incongruity helped me relax enough to take in the sounds and sights. Arik said we would sleep on the beach that night. That didn't worry me because I assumed it would be full of kids like us, who couldn't afford a hotel and didn't want to sleep at a hostel.

Feeling carefree, we walked around the city for a while. It never occurred to me to ask why we were there. It was easier to pretend that we were on vacation. I relaxed a bit as we walked. It felt really good to move, even though my body was exhausted and I was in pain. I had a skull-splitting headache, my shoulder hurt, and I suspected I was developing a urinary tract infection, but there was something about keeping my feet moving that helped me stay in the present. My weariness ebbed a little. As we walked past one of the souvenir shops, we heard a popular disco song playing inside. I was ecstatic to hear a song in English. I grabbed Arik's arm and we started singing the song together. He sang with the thickest, silliest accent I had ever heard. I could feel myself smiling from ear to ear listening to him sing, my head filling with sweet memories as I sang that song from home.

We had spent some of my $50 on bus rides and food, but Arik decided we had enough to go to a real restaurant for dinner. We sneaked into a youth hostel by the beach and took a shower. I couldn't believe how free I felt being in the shower alone, not being watched. Even though we hadn't paid, that small infraction didn't keep me from enjoying these little moments of freedom. This one didn't last long. As I was brushing my hair, Arik walked in. He didn't care that he was on the girls' side of the hostel. He told me to hurry up because we would be in trouble if we got caught. That seemed reasonable, so I let the anger I felt when he walked in on me subside.

We walked into the tourist center of town, to a restaurant that had white linen tablecloths and a full menu. This was the first restaurant I had been to in the Middle East. A part of me was in shock that there were actual sit-down restaurants in the country. Our mood was light. We ate an expensive meal and relaxed on the restaurant patio.

As it started to get dark, Arik's mood began to change. By now, I could easily pick up his non-verbal communication. I could tell when something was coming, giving me enough time to tighten my stomach, pull my shoulders forward, and steel myself before he said a word. He told me we were going to go to the beach to find a good spot before it filled up. He was extremely tense and his mood had changed quickly. My intuition told me that I had just eaten my last meal with him.

On the way to the beach, we passed some phone booths. I knew Arik kept some tokens in his pocket, and I asked him if I could call my mother. He got a nasty snarl on his face and said, "Sure." We walked to a booth, I took my mother's number out of my purse and Arik dialed the number for me. When she answered the phone, I told her where I was and said that I wanted to go home. I asked her, "Will you please help me get home?" Her one word answer before she hung up on me was, "No."

I was both crushed by her answer and furious with myself for calling her in the first place. I'm not sure why I called her; except for my foreboding at dinner with Arik. Maybe I wanted someone to know where I was, maybe I wanted to be rescued, or maybe I wanted to give her one last chance to prove she cared about me. Intellectually, I knew she would never help me, but my emotions had won out and pushed me to call. What upset me was that even though I knew she wouldn't help me, I still felt the sting of her rejection. I had been abandoned again. After everything she had done to me in my past and in that country, my stomach still turned over and sank. When I hung up the phone, Arik told me, "Come" and we walked silently to the beach.

It was surprisingly crowded with people our age. There was a lot of laughter and partying, and couples making love in their sleeping bags. We found a spot and laid out our bags. As we settled on the beach Arik pointed across the water and told me what country we were looking at. He told me that as we were looking at them, they were looking back at us. As we crawled into our sleeping bags, he told me to make sure that I keep my feet tucked up because thieves were known to come in the middle of the night and slice open bags to steal anything people stored at the bottom. He turned over and went to sleep. I barely slept that night. Not only was I afraid of getting my feet cut, but the beach was rocky and I still had a queasy feeling in my stomach that something awful was going to happen.

We woke up early the next morning and washed up at one of the beach restrooms. I had a terrible stomach ache and my body was sore and very stiff. I was hungry and crabby. I could feel my irritability building with each passing moment. I had reached the end of my rope and didn't want to hear anything Arik had to say to me that morning. It had been a long time since I had been insolent. I had forgotten my fear and was operating on weak adrenaline.

Arik came out of the bathroom wearing his military fatigues and I let out a sigh. I was right. This was going to be another day of unknown terror. The memory of our easy day of vacation fun dropped into the shadows as he walked up and told me to, "Come."

He led me to the market square and we sat on the steps. We were both hungry. We had spent all of the money I had in my purse the night before at the restaurant. We had no money for food or for a bus ticket back north. I felt helpless but angry too, as we sat on those steps. The square was filling up with noisy tourists. The buzz of their excitement, my growing hunger, and the exhaustion of the last nine days were quickly taking their toll. I could feel my anger boiling to the surface.

Arik got up, told me he would be right back and left me alone. With each passing minute, the heat seemed more intense and the crowd seemed noisier. He was only gone a short time, but when he came back and said, "Come," it was the last straw. I swung around, stood up, and starting yelling, "Stop treating me like a dog. I don't come to commands like a dog. I hate you and I hate this country. What's wrong with you people?" I ranted and stamped my feet, feeling completely out of control, exploding with pent-up frustration and fear.

I was enraged, but my body and senses were still on high alert. I felt someone coming up behind me. Before I could turn around, I was being firmly escorted out of the square by two soldiers. I watched as Arik simply turned around and walked away. All I could focus on was him walking away from me. He was leaving me! I was so hurt and angry that I didn't register that I was being put into a car.

Two military men, wearing different uniforms than I was used to seeing, were in the front seat. Alone in the back, I stared straight ahead. I didn't want to look out the windows in case I saw Arik on the street. I felt certain I would never see him or this country again.

Chapter 19
THE CAPSTONE MEMORY

I call the following piece of my story the Capstone Memory. I recalled it in my therapist's office on a hot July evening, three years before I remembered any other details of my experiences overseas. This memory spilled out as I sat across from Kevin. He let me talk without interruption until I was finished. I spoke with crystal clear intensity. For the past four years I haven't been able to write about this along with the earlier events of my story, because my visceral reactions would overwhelm me. I would dissociate. I am past that fear now, and it's important to honor this piece of my story. Unlike the preceding chapters, some of this one is written from a bird's-eye view. This was the 10th and final day of my journey overseas.

The soldiers were silent as we drove to a remote location not far from the market square. I sensed that we traveled for about thirty minutes. I believed they were taking me somewhere to kill me. I knew I had failed at everything they had asked me to do. I was sure they knew by now, that my psyche was severely damaged. After weeks of isolation in Quay, and all the other traumas since the tunnel, any shred of my psychological health had been obliterated. I was broken and I assumed that I was of no use to them.

We stopped at a cement structure that looked eerily like the one in the north, except there was no tower next to it. It was isolated and blended into the desert terrain. I followed the two soldiers into the building. The room we entered was fairly small and the lighting was dim compared to the bright, hot sun outside.

It felt stuffy and closed-in. The only furniture I saw was a table off to the left and a cot by the back wall.

Without any verbal exchange, the drivers left me with two men who had been waiting there. They looked hardened and intimidating. I felt helpless, filled with dread and terror. My heart was pounding so hard and fast that I thought it might explode out of my chest. The more frightening looking of the two spoke to me in good but heavily accented English. He told me to take off my clothes. I just stood there in shock. Losing his patience, he hit me in the face, knocking me down to the floor. I landed hard on the cement. Fear and adrenaline sent me crawling for safety against the wall.

Watching both men coming towards me, and overwhelmed with fear, I dissociated. When the white-hot explosions of pain coursed through my body and mind, I would do whatever it took to dissociate. At one point as I was going in and out of consciousness, I looked down at my body and told myself that I was torn apart. My arms and legs were broken off from my torso. I knew that I wouldn't feel pain if that was the case, so that's what I made myself believe.

From high above, I looked down on what was happening. I was separate from the girl who was being tortured on the floor. I watched the horrific ways they beat and abused her body. I could see and hear what they were doing to her. I could see them taking pride in their work. Eventually, I saw her pass out from the shock and pain. When they were done torturing her, she lay still on the floor for a long while, and finally belly-crawled to the cot. When she lay down on the cot, I let part of myself rejoin her.

I don't know how long I was passed out on the cot. When I woke up, I was shivering. It was either dark in the room or my eyes were swollen shut from tears and bruising. I rolled off the cot and crawled as close as I could to the wall on the far side of the room, making sure I was turned away from the door. My insides were aching and numb at the same time. I was desperately thirsty; felt the thickness of my tongue and swollen lips.

Lying on the cement floor, I thought I heard the sound of a cat mewing. It took a while to dawn on me that the mewing was actually coming from me. It was the only sound that my weak and damaged body could make.

I knew that I was dying. I didn't want to die alone. I had lived my whole life without anyone caring about my safety or well-being. I was unloved, but I no longer felt any pain. With darkness enveloping me and thinking I was taking my final breaths, my last thought was that no one would ever find me. I would be lost forever.

Chapter 20
HOME

I must have been unconscious when they moved me to the place where I now know that I spent six weeks recovering. I don't recall a lot of my convalescence. I have snippets of women coming in and out of my room attending to my physical needs but that's about it. I don't remember any doctors standing next to my bed discussing my conditions or what treatments I needed, and I don't recall nurses making small talk with me as I lay there day after day.

What I do remember were the recurring nightmares and daytime reliving of what had happened to me that previous month. I relived the tunnel and the day of the explosion. I dreamt of the woods, and of the chaos and brutality there. I had dreams of the man putting his hand on my face and telling me how much I had disappointed them. But mostly I relived being tortured over and over again. No one came in to talk to me about what happened, or help me with the nightmares or flashbacks. It's hard to articulate the pain and suffering of being locked up with my memories; reliving them day and night, isolated and alone. I wasn't able to process those horrors with anyone.

As I began to feel better, I spent a fair amount of time out of bed, sitting in a chair. I was in a comfortable room with soft yellow walls. Between the language the nurses and doctors were speaking and the landscape outside my window, I knew I was no longer in the Middle East. But I was hyper-vigilant and cowered when anyone came near me, terrified of being touched. I knew my body felt pain as it healed, but I didn't want to feel any connection to it. I remember the powerful relief of not being thirsty any longer. That was the only connection I allowed myself to feel with any part of me. I healed slowly, and in silence. Quiet, alone, afraid of human touch, and hopeless.

A woman came into my room one day and told me it was time to go. I accepted her help getting dressed because I still felt incredibly stiff and sore. I could barely lift my arms, and my torso and legs felt deeply bruised. I was soon weak and light-headed from the effort of moving. After putting on a dress, I washed my face, brushed my teeth, and the woman brushed my hair. It felt strange doing basic self-care in front of a mirror. I wasn't connected to my body so it seemed as if I was acting out a play. With each movement, I told myself I never wanted to feel this way again, and I would go to any lengths to prevent it.

The woman led me downstairs. It seemed as if we were in a house, but with a colder feel to it. It was a large and very old building, rich and grand but completely different than any place I had been so far. The air felt damp and humid. With beautiful paneling on the walls and rugs covering the dark wood floors, this place had a sturdy and historic feel to it.

For a moment, I thought I was back in America, in something like my aunt and uncle's house in Philadelphia. I was snapped back to reality quickly though, by my body. My feet and legs were stiff and I felt unsteady as we made our way down the stairs. Somewhere in my brain I heard a comforting voice telling me everything would be okay because we were on the move again.

The woman led me to a large set of wooden doors and knocked softly. The door opened and I stepped inside the room, and the woman was gone. I stood there shaken, as I saw a group of six or eight men sitting around a massive wooden table. I felt a flicker of surprise because I recognized two of the men from years ago at the facility. Back then, I only knew them as the name "sirs." Today, they are recognizable to most Americans. I felt myself go cold with terror.

The power in the room was palpable. It quickly dawned on me that these were the men who were truly controlling my life. A lot of my questions suddenly had answers. I knew on some deep level, that my life was not really being orchestrated by raping, torturing men from a foreign country, but by this sinister group that thrived on power.

The two American men barely glanced in my direction and didn't say a word to me. The man at the head of the table addressed me. He stood up and directed me to come to him. As I walked toward him, fear coursed through my body. My legs shook with each step.

He said that they were surprised that I was so inept and weak. He said, "*Surely*, you must know that we spent a lot of time on you, and you proved no good for the job." He continued, "However, there is loyalty to your family so we may find something for you to do." And then it was suddenly over. I was dismissed. In answer to his almost imperceptible nod, the door opened and a man came to take me away. I had probably been in that room less than three minutes.

As I was walked out of there, I felt humiliated, small, and ashamed for letting them down. But I also felt threatened. Fear was settling in like concrete. I followed the man out of the room and down some stairs. It felt as if we were going underground and I was afraid that I was being taken into another tunnel.

We came into a cold hallway with gray walls. As we walked down the hallway, this man explained to me in terrifying terms how I must *never* talk about anything that happened since I had been away from home. While he spoke, he gave me a list of directives which were obvious threats. Each word had the same meaning. "Don't talk. Don't speak to anyone, ever, about anything." I was overwhelmed with anxiety and had a panic attack as we neared the door. I could tell it led to the outside, and I was terrified thinking that I was going to be thrown out into the street alone, without any money. I would rather be with people who tortured me than be abandoned. As we got closer to the door, the man grabbed me and holding me tight, hissed in my right ear, "No matter where you live, or how many years pass we will always see you, your friends, and your future children, and we will know if you have talked." He ended his terrifying delivery with, "And if you *do* talk, then my Little One, you will be killed." The heat of his breath and the severity of his threat landed in my ear, but settled in my soul.

When he opened the door, there was a black car waiting for me. I got into the back seat as I was told, and we sped away. I began to look closely at the buildings we were passing. My father had spent a lot of time in Europe on business, and had described many of the cities in detail to me. I had seen pictures of some of these buildings. He had spoken about one of them that had many stairs. He told us how one day, as he was rushing out, he had tumbled down the steps. A nice lady had helped him up and invited him over for dinner that night. I wondered if this was that same city. I realized that nothing that happened in my life had been random bad luck. I wasn't just a person born under a black cloud, I was a person born into a dreadful family.

The car stopped in front of a small airport. I got out, shut the door behind me and didn't look back. I knew I had no ticket, no luggage and no passport, but bone weary and confused, I did the only thing that made sense to me. I sat down and stared into space. I wasn't going to risk talking to anyone. I had just been threatened with my life, for the rest of my life. I sat down and stared off into the nothingness, exhausted and sick.

Before long, a couple approached me and said they were there to help me. They had a ticket and a passport. The woman held my arm and helped me stand up. She said we were going to go to the bathroom to get cleaned up and that I would be traveling with them. She told me that my luggage would be waiting for me when we get off the plane, but I didn't believe her. I thought that she was going to take me somewhere else to be hurt. But in truth, it didn't matter what she said. By this point, I was going to follow any direction I was given. As I got off the chair to follow her, I turned around and looked back at where I had been sitting, picturing myself still sitting in that chair. Somewhere in my emotionally broken mind, I was choosing to leave myself behind at the airport. I knew it was my only chance for survival. In my mind, as I walked away I left the little, broken, twenty-year-old girl at this small airport in Europe. I left that abandoned part of me sitting in a chair holding all my secrets. I turned around and followed the woman into the bathroom.

The couple and I got onto a small plane and flew to a larger airport. True to the woman's word, my luggage and documents were waiting for me. I took my luggage, went into the bathroom and put on my own jeans, shirt, sweater, socks and shoes. There was something about wearing my own clothes that helped me begin to repress everything. I suddenly felt a sense of self again. These were my clothes, ones that I had bought and paid for with my own money. I hadn't seen them since we left Quay. I didn't know how long ago it had been since I lived in isolation with Arik, but in my mind it seemed like years. Putting on my own clothes helped me begin to push the reality of my recent past far enough away that I suddenly found myself looking forward to going home.

We boarded a plane to New York. When the plane took off, I rested my head against the window. I was reasonably sure that nothing was going to happen on the flight, so I let myself relax and start to believe that it had all been a dream. Towards the end of the flight, the woman told me that they would be in touch. She explained that I was going to marry Arik in order to bring him to America. She told me that after a few years, if I wished, we could divorce. She said that he and I needed to begin a campaign of letter-writing to prove our feelings for one another and show that our love was real.

As sick and tired as my brain was, I understood that this was my new assignment. They had, in fact, found something else for me to do. This wasn't a dream and I wasn't out of their clutches. My mind was firing white hot flares of disbelief as I tried to take in what this woman was saying. I think she had waited until the end of our flight to deliver all this, so I couldn't let it sink in and make a fuss. But my body reacted immediately and I threw up.

When we landed in New York she handed me another ticket, told me where the baggage claim was, and that she would be in touch. I stood like a statue as she walked away. Even though I had just met her, I felt abandoned. I was overwhelmed by feelings of being thrown away like garbage, disregarded, forgotten, and left completely alone.

I went to the baggage claim, got my brown suitcase, and found a bank of chairs in a quiet part of the terminal. My flight back home wasn't leaving for a few hours, so I curled up on the seats and fell asleep. As I drifted off, I realized that the only language I was hearing over the loud speakers was English. The arrival and departure information sounded like a sweet lullaby, and I slept.

The flight back to Minnesota was uneventful. I went to a pay phone, called my roommate Grace, and asked if she would pick me up at the airport. She was cheerful and surprised to hear my voice. Grace excitedly told me she would be there in about an hour. It was shocking to have someone genuinely happy to hear from me. I can't explain how confusing that was. I was so used to being mistreated that I met any kindness with mistrust.

I had no idea what the day or date was, but I was stunned by the cold and snowy landscape outside the airport. When I had left for the Middle East, it was summer. Now the snow beyond Grace's car windows lay dirty, as if it had been there for months. I asked her what month it was and why there was so much snow. She laughed and said it was December. Except for the three days at home between my first and second trip overseas, I had been gone for more than four months.

I felt dizzy and nauseous realizing how long I had been away. I had lost all concept of time. As I watched the Midwestern landscape rush by, I willed myself to feel relief that I was safely back home. When we pulled into the driveway of our duplex, I finally let myself exhale a little bit. I had made it to my house. I brought my suitcase in, found my cat Carlotta and held her for as long as she would let me. I went to my room and lay down on my bed. It still had the same cat sheets on it from the day I left all those months ago, and I fell into a heavy sleep.

I knew deep down, that in spite of wishing I was dead so many times during the last four months, I was happy to be alive. I didn't cry, I didn't thank God that I was alive, and I didn't thank my handlers for sparing my life. Instead, I took an anticlimactic nap in the middle of the afternoon in my own bed, with my cat purring at my feet.

PART 3

Chapter 21
STARTING OVER

My first few weeks after returning home were a blur as tried to I re-acclimate. I was shut down emotionally and wouldn't answer any questions about where I had been. I was trying to metabolize my memories from overseas, and at the same time finding it difficult to believe that what happened to me while I was there was real. Earlier in my life, I had been able to convince myself that the abuse I endured couldn't have been real. That was how I coped. But this time, as I was trying to repress what happened, I began to doubt and question my every thought and every experience.

I still felt physically battered and bruised. I felt emotionally traumatized, confused, and terrified. I was all alone with my thoughts and memories, and continually having flashbacks or nightmares. My stomach never stopped hurting and I felt like I had a bladder infection. I had terrible pains in my shoulder and hip, and I felt so sick overall that I spent most of my time lying down. I probably should have gone to a doctor, but there was no way I was going to let an adult touch my body.

Every time the phone rang, I was sick with worry that it would be someone telling me to get back on a plane. I was desperately trying to figure out how to act the part that was assigned to me, that I had fallen in love and wanted to bring my boyfriend to America.

I felt totally alone, but I also knew that I needed to find a job to make money. I had experience working in group homes with developmentally disabled children, so I started there. I didn't feel comfortable telling my roommate Grace that I didn't have any money, because I was afraid she would kick me out. I picked up the Yellow Pages, flipped to the Social Services section and began calling down the list. My self esteem was non-existent and I couldn't imagine anyone wanting to hire me, but needing money to keep me and my cat fed and housed, forced me to put on a fake smile and go to interviews.

I was lucky enough to find a place fairly close to my house that was hiring. Within a week of returning home I had found a job working with adults that had emotional and behavior disorders and autism. I was suffering from enormous Posttraumatic Stress Disorder symptoms, including flashbacks, hyper-vigilance, anxiety and nightmares, and the stress of my new job fed my worsening symptoms. The clients were aggressive on a daily basis; often hitting, spitting, screaming and acting out. The noise of their screams and their physical outbursts would send me into fierce flashbacks.

I could barely hold myself together against the demands of the job. I was moody and depressed, having a hard time handling any kind of authority figure. I didn't want to do anything my boss asked me to do. I figured any person in authority was trying to control my life. I didn't trust them. I was constantly looking over my shoulder, waiting for someone to drag me away from my work, put me on a plane and find me a new job in a foreign country.

I worked weekdays until 3:30, and then went straight home to crash. But, as the weeks and months wore on, and I slowly grew more accustomed to living with the stress and the fear, I fell into a routine. I connected with my friend Mary, got closer with my roommate Grace, and began to go out and party. I drank and smoked weed as often as I could. I started going to parties and bars to pick up men. Sometimes I would find a guy who was willing to be my boyfriend for a week or two, but most of them would quickly tire of my crazy need for control. The truth was that I felt completely out of control myself, and more suicidal every day. I would often hide out in my room hoping no one would notice I was home. But I was miserable whether I was alone or with people.

I found myself waking up every night and looking out my window into the strand of trees behind our duplex. I saw men running through the woods and shooting guns. They were wearing the same military uniforms and using the same weapons I had seen in the Middle East. That same scenario played out every single night in my back yard. It never occurred to me to ask my roommate if she heard or saw anything. It never occurred to me that I might be having flashbacks. I just assumed that Grace, or whoever was sleeping next to me was a heavy sleeper, or that they simply didn't care that people were being shot at outside our window.

I began to build even more walls around myself. I wouldn't engage in any kind of conversation that I thought would turn personal. If someone asked about my past or my family, I was an expert at deflecting the conversation back to them. I became a master at making myself unmemorable, and gave only vague answers about anything personal.

Even though I was finding a groove with my new life, I was keeping a fierce eye on the news and any mention of the Middle East. I would turn on the TV and walk to the back of the room behind the couch, using it as a shield. I was anxious and terrified watching the news stories. When the program was over, I would gingerly walk to the TV, turn it off, and back away, ready to retreat to my darkened room. I went to sleep every night wondering if tomorrow would be the day that I'd be sent back to that part of the world.

I knew I was living on borrowed time. My assignment with Arik was weighing heavily on me. I remembered the hissed threat in my ear, and I didn't feel safe anywhere I went. I didn't know when the next part of my life would begin or end. I just knew I would never be safe again.

About a month after I got home, I received a letter from Arik. He called me his little sweetheart and told me about what he had been doing since I left. It was obvious that Arik hadn't written the letter. I knew that he could barely speak English, but in his letter he had great command over the language. He even had legible handwriting and perfect punctuation. As I read it, chills crept up my spine and settled in my chest. I was sick with fear and didn't know how to handle it. So I ignored it.

I couldn't force myself to write to him. I hoped that if I didn't write back, they would forget about me. I tried to convince myself that if I didn't write back, that it would have been all a dream. Unconsciously, I was desperately trying to gain some control over my life.

A few weeks after Arik's letter came I received an envelope with no return address. Even though I had no idea who it was from, I knew I had to open it. It was from the couple on the plane who left me in New York, asking me how things were going, and if I written back to my sweetheart. They said it was important to let him know how much I missed and loved him, and that I wanted to marry him. I didn't know how they got my address or knew that I had gotten a letter from Arik.

I felt like I had no choice, so I went to the post office and bought stamps, some airmail stationary and began my letter-writing campaign with Arik. My letters were always short. I never told him where I worked or what I did in my spare time. I told him I was fine and asked him about his life.

I was literally afraid to stop writing, so the correspondence between the two of us became more regular. But whenever a letter came, I would either break out in itchy, red hives or throw up. After a year of our writing back and forth, I started to taper off my replies. I hadn't received any more letters from the New York couple, so I assumed they had disappeared from my life.

When I stopped my regular replies to Arik's letters, he got angry. He pressed me to write, and asked why I had stopped corresponding. I realized that I enjoyed the anger in his letters. He seemed really bothered by the fact that I was ignoring him. The longer I was away from Arik, the less I was afraid of him. I found some pleasure in his anger because I knew that there was no way he could personally hurt me. After all, he was on the other side of the world. So, after fifteen months of corresponding, I completely stopped writing.

I went on with my life. I was learning to cope a little better at work. I was making new friends and filling my evenings and weekends with partying as hard as I could. I was doing everything in my power to repress my past and build impenetrable walls between myself and anyone who wanted to get close to me.

A few months after I stopped writing, I received a phone call from Arik. He told me he was coming to America in a few days. I remember standing in my kitchen stunned, saying, "Don't come here!" But he told me he already had his ticket and I needed to pick him up at the airport. I told him again, "No, don't come." I wasn't sure where that courage came from, but the guy that I had just started dating was standing next to me. Somehow, seeing him there gave me courage. I felt protected.

Arik called me again a few days later and told me he had landed in Ohio. I told him again, "Don't come to me," and hung up. That was our last phone conversation, and we never exchanged letters again. I thought I'd never see him again.

I was thunderstruck when three years later, as I sat outside my workplace, Arik casually walked across the street, right up to me, and said, "You got fat."

Chapter 22
I'M GETTING MARRIED

I met my future husband in an Irish pub about sixteen months after returning home. I had gone out that night with some people from work who had taken me under their wings. We walked into the small bar, found a seat in the back and settled in for the night. Across the room, I noticed a thin boy with long brown hair who was dressed in a suit. He looked totally out of place in that suit but he seemed comfortable and relaxed. He was having a good time. I didn't notice what music was playing or if my friends tried to talk to me, because I was transfixed on this guy sitting across the room. I couldn't take my eyes off him. Every now and then we would make eye contact, and he would smile slightly. When my friends decided to call it a night and as we got up to leave, I walked up to the cute guy in the suit, gave him my phone number and told him my name.

All the way home I lamented to my friend, that I had probably just given my name to a rapist, and that I was going to be his next victim. I told them if I wasn't at work on Monday it was probably because he had murdered me. I made them promise to give my cat to my roommate. It was crazy talk, but my friends sat quietly and let me rant. For some reason I was feeling out of control, and couldn't wait to get home and out of their car.

His name was Jay, and he called me the next day. We made plans to meet at the same pub the following weekend. I enlisted four of my friends to go with me, and on Friday my friends and I had our first date with him. Jay and I talked nonstop about everything, while my friends enjoyed the band. I was instantly attracted to him. He had a hard, dangerous edge about him. I felt comfortable with danger, so he was exactly what I wanted. He came back to our apartment and our first date turned into a whole weekend.

We quickly became inseparable. I would pick Jay up on Friday after work and drop him off at his apartment in the city on Sunday evenings. As I got to know him, I learned that he was as emotionally damaged as I was. The difference was that he was actively trying to heal and make a better life for himself, while I was still psychologically and emotionally bleeding on the inside. I was living under the threat that I might be called back overseas, and I was still writing back and forth with Arik. I was trying to find a way to deny my past. I liked this man and knew that I couldn't risk sharing any of it with him.

One of the things I appreciated in the early part of our relationship was that Jay was so intent on healing his own wounds, that he didn't ask any probing questions. He was actively trying to make amends, and trying to figure out how to escape the cycle of poverty and abuse that he grew up in, so he accepted anything I said at face value. By not prying, Jay unknowingly helped me develop the opaque scrim that I hid behind for the next twenty-eight years.

I was Jay's ticket out of the inner city. He desperately wanted to change his life. With me, he could practice how to talk with people who didn't speak street slang. I also had a nice apartment in the suburbs and I was his golden opportunity to morph into a new person. He was honest with me from the start, and told me he was using me for a chance at a better life. He said that he didn't want a serious relationship. I didn't care; I never expected to have a real relationship, with anyone, ever.

For me, Jay was a bodyguard. I felt threatened all the time and I needed someone to provide physical protection. I didn't pine for flowers or love letters; I craved protection. We both needed a lifeline as we crafted new identities. We were both constantly changing and growing. We became best friends. Since we had no expectations of our relationship, we could both afford to be vulnerable without fear of judgment, and never forget to let loose and have fun. We struck an easy balance between the drudgery of our lives and having fun.

I never let myself have feelings for anyone before I met Jay. I didn't know what love felt like. I didn't know how to give or receive respect, and I never dreamt of marriage or children. Frankly, I didn't think those options were open to me. I was just trying to survive until I was killed. I was always waiting. I assumed that Jay would stop wanting to be with me, and then leave. But he came back every weekend and we eventually went from friendship to dating.

About a month after we started dating, I got the phone call from Arik telling me he was coming to America. Jay was standing in the kitchen with me while I was on the phone. I turned around and looked at Jay, and courageously thought maybe I had a chance at another life. That's when and why I said, "No, don't come." I let myself smile with gratification when I hung up the phone. I told Jay who I had been talking to and said, "I didn't want Arik to come because I don't want to mess things up with my new boyfriend." That was the first time I had ever called anyone "my boyfriend." Jay didn't seem to mind the title. So, at the age of twenty-two, I had my first boyfriend.

I asked people at work how to be a girlfriend. I got a lot of advice about lingerie, makeup, and what meals to cook. I had never related to any male except sexually, so all this advice was as foreign and challenging for me as learning a new language. But I was determined to learn how to do the normal everyday things a girlfriend did for someone.

I went to a department store to learn how to put on make-up. I bought sexy lingerie, and looked up recipes to make romantic meals. I felt uncomfortable and uneasy. I was trying to become someone who was "normal" but I was still the same threatened girl, just waiting to be called back overseas or killed. I became more and more irritable. I hated trying to become "a girl next door" just to get a boy to stay. I had a tough enough time pretending that I hadn't come from a life of abuse, torture, and abandonment and now, I felt I had to be some made-up, 1950's version of the perfect girlfriend. I was becoming tense and crabby, but willing to do those things if it meant I was being a good girlfriend.

It turned out Jay didn't like make-up. When I came out of the bathroom all dolled-up, he seemed angry. Instead of saying that I looked pretty, he said he didn't understand why I thought I had to paint my face in order for him to think I was beautiful. I felt both devastated and angry. By not happily acknowledging my new look, I thought he was trying to control me and my life. I burst into a rage at him, screaming, "Never tell me what to do again!" I stamped around the apartment aggravated and hurt. From my damaged perspective, Jay had just turned into Arik telling me I was stupid, ugly, and fat. Jay apologized, and explained that he liked me just the way I was. He did like the sexy bedroom clothes however, and I enjoyed learning to cook. I started collecting recipes and ditched the heavy make-up; it felt awful on my skin anyway.

As our relationship grew more serious, I grew more ill-at-ease. My friends liked Jay but I knew my family. If they ever met him, they would judge and despise him. He came from a poor up-bringing. He spoke unpolished English, had terrible grammar, and used a lot of slang. We were polar opposites in the way we looked at the world. He saw the American dream and hoped to grab that brass ring, and I was cynical and leery of the rich and powerful.

Our courtship was not without its struggles. We were both growing and changing rapidly. Jay was ready to take giant leaps. He had boundless hope for what his future could be. He was ready to find his identity, make a good living, and contribute to society. I was ready to morph into anyone but myself, or not have an identity at all. I wanted to escape any reminders of my past. Because Jay was so obsessed with making a better life for himself, he was always satisfied with the answers I gave him about my life before I met him. His past was terrible so he wasn't eager to relive those details either. So the less we asked about each other, the better it was for both of us. We were a perfect dysfunctional couple. We were young, naïve, and heading toward an eventual lack-of-communication disaster.

Jay moved in with me and Grace about nine months after we started dating. Grace and Jay became close friends. They loved partying and staying up late talking with each other. The three of us were perfect roommates. A month after Jay moved in, while I was standing next to the same phone where I told Arik not to come, Jay got down on one knee and asked me to marry him. Shocked and excited, I said, "Yes!" He put the ring on my finger; I hugged him, and then I instantly panicked. I felt sick and I came down with a fierce urinary tract infection. I somehow knew that this had to be brought on by old emotional wounds.

I let down my guard when I said yes to his marriage proposal, but now, I heard the hiss of the threat in my ear, reminding me that I would be killed if I ever talked about anything that had happened to me. How could I be over-the-moon ecstatic that I was engaged and at the same time terrified by the pain and flashbacks? I managed to get a prescription over the phone for my UTI. The next day, after a couple doses of antibiotics and a lot of hard work pushing down my pain and fear, I felt better. I started to let myself feel some joy every time I looked at the ring on my finger.

I was nervous about Jay meeting my family, and was nervous to meet his. I didn't know what marriage meant, or how it would change our relationship. I was in love with Jay and he was my best friend, but I didn't trust him. I didn't trust anyone.

I began to do everything I could to make Jay's life miserable so he would break our engagement and abandon me. I needed him to fulfill my fears. I thought if I could make it happen myself, then it would be easier to handle the pain. But he was unmoved by my needling and nagging. He loved me and wanted to make a life with me. He wanted marriage, the house, kids, a nice job and a comfortable life. I was afraid to want any of those things. All I wanted was to stay alive.

When we fought, Jay simply got angry, said what he had to say, and got over it. He cooled down, let it go and went on with life. He didn't hold grudges, he didn't use my words against me, and he didn't threaten me. He just let things roll off his back and moved on to the next moment. Jay learned to do that in his therapeutic healing process. He worked hard to put his dark demons to rest before he settled down.

I was always waiting to be abandoned, to be abused. I was waiting to be thrown away and I was waiting to be killed. I never thought that someone could get angry and still like me, let alone love me. I pushed him away as often as I pulled him close. I was still running the tape that I was a disgusting animal who was unworthy of love. I couldn't let go of the feeling that I was insignificant and disposable. It never occurred to me that someone would want to spend their life with me, so I couldn't fully give my love and trust to Jay.

I settled down and somehow convinced myself that Jay would be safe if we got married. We set the date. None of my friends were married at the time, so I went to the women at work to find out how to plan a wedding. They told me that I needed to find a dress, a venue, decide on flowers, music, food, bridesmaids and all the other trappings that went into planning a wedding. Neither Jay nor I was the least bit interested in anything they suggested.

We decided we wanted a small outdoor wedding, speaking vows we had written ourselves. So seven months after our engagement we had a beautiful ceremony on a crisp October day. The wedding and reception was small, but the party afterwards was an all night blow-out. We all had a great time until sunrise. It was the perfect wedding for us. To this day, we still visit the gazebo where we said our vows.

We lived with our roommate Grace for six months after we married. This was the apartment I came home to after being in the Middle East, so I was afraid to leave it behind. But knowing that married couples should start their life on their own, after much trepidation, Jay, my cat, and I moved out to begin our life together. For some wonderful reason, almost as soon as we were off on our own, I found it easier and easier to repress my past. But the effects of my trauma didn't care that I was married or had moved to another apartment. They would start to affect every single aspect of my new life.

Chapter 23
THE NEXT FOUR YEARS

Moving out of the apartment that we shared with Grace stirred up enormous fears in me. I didn't want to leave the home that had been my refuge when I came back from overseas. I didn't want to move away from my roommate. Grace had been a constant presence in my life since I came back, and I was afraid I would never see her again, that she would forget about me. I now know that line of thinking is a sign of an attachment disorder, which is one of the biggest effects the trauma had on me.

I had no insight into how damaged I was by the trauma. I was trying to repress and forget my past, and living in survival mode day after day. I hadn't been to a therapist and I couldn't see the impact my behavior or distorted thinking had on anyone else. The more I suppressed my reality, the more I related in unhealthy and psychologically damaging ways. So, instead of talking to Grace about my feelings, I became irritable and argumentative.

In the four years Grace and I lived together we had never had a fight or spoken a cross word to one another. As the move got closer, I became moody and irrational. She and I found ourselves arguing over little things. It wasn't Grace it was me trying to push her away, before she could walk away. A week before Jay and I moved out, Grace and I got into a huge argument over which one of us owned a pan. She insisted it was hers and I insisted it was mine. We wound up saying some very hurtful things to each other, so hurtful that we didn't talk for six months after I moved out.

I was devastated and didn't know what to do. Knowing Grace as well as I did, I guessed she felt the same way. Months later, as I was going through a box of pictures, I found a photo of the two of us together. I mailed it to her and that was enough to break the ice. We got together for coffee, made up, and in the thirty years since haven't had an argument like that again. Those six months of silence and separation affected us both deeply, and we found a way to communicate respectfully.

The truth behind my fear of moving was that I was unprepared to live with a man. My only experience was with Arik. I was terrified Jay was going to lock me away in a tiny little apartment in the middle of nowhere, and my nightmare of isolation would begin all over again.

I fell into a deep depression after we moved and I started to regret getting married. Neither Jay nor I had any idea how to work at a relationship. He was still going through a lot of personal and emotional changes. He was adapting to the reality of living in the suburbs for the first time in his life, and we were both trying to figure out how to be a couple. We did the best we could and like most newlyweds we muddled through a difficult first year of marriage.

For our first anniversary we decided to visit my sister. She lived on a beautiful island and I thought that the sun would help my depressed mood. My older sister had always been a powerfully manipulative force in my life, so I was on edge whenever I spoke with her. She had been judgmental about Jay, making comments to me about his upbringing. But I pushed to visit her because we could stay for free. A week in paradise quickly became a miserable trip for both of us.

Lucy was having a mental health crisis and spent the entire week in bed, crying. I was agitated and nervous as soon as we landed. When I was younger, I had spent some summers on the island with her and those bad memories flooded back in. To make matters worse, it turned out that Jay was terrified of the ocean. We tried to make the best of it by visiting some tourist attractions and hiking in the mountains, but our getaway ended up being stressful and expensive.

We couldn't wait to get back home. As I was boarding the plane I told myself that I would never go back to that island again. There were triggers everywhere. I felt like I couldn't share what I was recalling with Jay, because I was doing everything I could to erase my past. I felt bad for Jay. Our "honeymoon" turned into a miserable week of ocean fears, crazy sister-in-law behavior, and an even more depressed wife.

A few months after we got back from our trip, I woke up with a terrible pain on my right side. I went to work, trying to hide my symptoms, but I was feverish and sweating. One of my co-workers took me aside and asked me if I was feeling okay. I told her I had some pain on my right side and it was getting worse. It never occurred to me to go to the doctor. She sent me home where I waited for Jay. When he got there, he immediately called the doctor who told us to go to an emergency room. I had appendicitis that needed surgery.

There was no way that I was going into an operating room. The last time I had been wheeled into an operating room, I was fourteen, and being forced into an abortion. I panicked. Not only was I having flashbacks about the abortion, but I was reliving the torture from overseas. Bouncing from one flashback to another, I dissociated. I woke up in the recovery room not remembering anything.

I was terrified when I opened my eyes. I was in post-surgical pain and feeling drugged and foggy. I became frantic and started lashing out because I couldn't figure out where I was. I must have been given a sedative because the next thing I knew I was back in my hospital room and heavily medicated. When I was released from the hospital, I knew I was in psychological trouble.

I was weak and traumatized from the emergency surgery and my flashbacks increased. The horror was that I didn't know they were flashbacks. The fragile control that I had over my life since the Middle East was unraveling, and I felt my mental health slipping away.

Jay had an accident at work while I was still recovering from surgery. One of the ovens in his plastics factory caught on fire. The flames exploded outward and Jay suffered 2nd degree burns on his face, neck, and hand. Somehow, we nursed one another through. When he came home from the hospital, Jay had made up his mind to change careers. He decided to go to school to become a stockbroker. I fully supported his decision. I knew that Jay associated success with a white collar job.

Jay's program kept him away from home for twelve hours a day. Neither of us understood how emotionally fragile I was, or that my being alone for so long every day would create problems. I was having constant flashbacks and felt out of control.

I had craved routine ever since I'd come back for overseas. I needed it to hold myself together, to feel some control over my life. I soon became obsessed with exercise and my weight. I had always been active and never weighed more than 115 pounds, but somehow in my mind, I decided that I was too heavy, and became obsessed with how I looked.

I began weighing myself at least five times a day. My daily food intake would sometimes be a single peach, and I exercised obsessively. I lost weight very fast and started to get sick. If I tried to put anything more than a peach in my stomach, I would throw up. I was dizzy and weak but couldn't stop myself.

One afternoon I was so weak that I could barely form a cohesive thought. Jay came home, and immediately took me to the doctor's office. We found out that my blood pressure had bottomed out. I was rushed to the emergency room and admitted to the hospital. I was distressed and uncooperative. I didn't care that I was starving myself and I didn't care that I weighed less than 95 pounds. But when I saw the panic in Jay's face, I calmed down and allowed the nurse to insert an IV.

When my doctor came the next day, he told me I couldn't leave the hospital until I weighed 100 pounds. I was medicated to keep me calm and quiet. After five days and with my promising to eat, my doctor relented and discharged me even though I weighed only 98 pounds. As soon as we got home, Jay threw out the scale and has never allowed one in our home again.

On a follow-up visit to my doctor, both he and I knew something was going on with me that I was unwilling or unable to talk about it. I was falling apart emotionally; I was irritable, hyper-vigilant, and becoming convinced that someone was going to take my husband away and kill him. I thought I was going crazy. My doctor was concerned and offered to walk me to a psychologist's office down the hall, but I declined. I knew that I would neither talk to nor trust anyone.

It was the end of winter and spring was fast approaching. As I left my doctor's office, I calmed myself with visions of sitting in the warm sunshine. I tamped down my fears and convinced myself that all I needed was to feel the sun on my face and everything would be okay.

I managed to go back to work. One warm spring day, while sitting outside with my coworkers, I saw someone walking across the street toward us. Before my brain could even register who it was, my stomach clenched, my chest constricted and my heart began pounding in my chest. It was Arik. It had been three years since I had seen him, and I hadn't talked to him in over two. Yet, there he was, walking straight towards me. He came out of thin air, as if he had just materialized. He crossed the street confidently as if he knew exactly where he was, and that he belonged there.

My mind was racing. How had he found me? Where did he come from? I couldn't comprehend what was happening when he suddenly walked up and said, "You got fat." I remember looking down at my red and white gingham shirt, and instantly hating it. I would never wear that shirt again. Even though I couldn't comprehend how or why he was standing there, what registered and permeated every cell in my body was his nasty comment. I instantly hated myself and the clothes I was wearing.

Arik was carrying a black backpack, which made my stomach turn with horrible memories. I told him to wait outside while I called my husband. I told Jay that Arik had come to visit and that I would be bringing him home. I felt completely outside myself; an observer watching and listening to someone else make the phone call.

Jay reminded me that he had plans to go out of town. I heard myself saying, "Don't cancel, just go, everything will be okay." It was one of the most surreal moments of my life. I was frightened to my very core, but I heard myself telling the one person that I thought could protect me, to stay away. My mind refused to work. I was on a weird sort of autopilot. I hung up the phone, went outside, led Arik to my car and we drove away. I didn't introduce him to any of my coworkers. I'm sure they were wondering who he was and why I was acting so strange.

We drove to my house without saying a word to each other. I didn't want to know why he was there or even how he found me. I was numb. When we got home, I went into my bedroom with our two cats, locked my door, and didn't come out until the next morning. Arik didn't knock on the door. He waited in my living room for me to come out.

The next morning, I saw that he had made himself at home. He had cooked dinner the night before and was lying on the couch reading a book. I finally asked him why he was there. He said, "To show you, you could be found anytime and anywhere." I asked him what he did when I told him not to come that day. He said he went to Ohio for a couple of weeks and then back to the Middle East.

He told me that he was hungry. I didn't want to cook for him, so we got in my car and went to a fast food restaurant. In a daze, I started driving us around. We drove for hours because I didn't want him in my house again. I didn't have anything to say to him, and he didn't seem interested in talking to me either. If the only purpose for his visit was the shock factor, it had worked and his job was done.

Finally, I ran out of places to drive and we went back to my house. I gathered up my cats and went back into the bedroom, locking the door behind me. When I came out the next morning, it was clear he was getting ready to leave. As I watched him pack up his things, he asked me what my husband did for a living. I told him he was going to school to become a stock broker. He grabbed my left hand, looked at my wedding ring and said, "He isn't anything like me." I felt ice travel through my body and down my spine. My only response was, "Yeah, I'm glad." And that was it. He left. He closed the door, walked down the street and was gone.

Arik was with me for about 36 hours. We probably said a total of five sentences to each other. After I was sure he was gone, I frantically cleaned my house to remove any trace of him, went into the bathroom and threw up, and waited for Jay to come home.

When he got home that evening and asked how my weekend was, all I said was, "Fine." I kept all our conversation about what he had done while he was out of town. I shut down any talk he wanted to have about Arik's visit. I never saw Arik again. Over the next four years, he would call once in a while to say, "Just calling to say hi." I hung up on him every time, which I imagined just made him smile.

About a year after Arik's visit, we moved into an old duplex in the city. I started a new job at a group home and somehow my mind was able to erase my existence before age 21. But I was suffering. I was irritable, moody and had terrible screaming nightmares nearly every night. If Jay was late coming home, I became hysterical thinking that someone had killed him. When he pressed me about my nightmares, or who I thought was going to hurt him, I could never answer, and would shut down emotionally.

I was reliving a terribly familiar loss of control over my life as I tried to manage waves of pain, sadness, and fear. I began to starve myself, and exercise excessively again. I became severely dehydrated and very sick from the weight loss, and found myself once again being rushed to the hospital. Just like before, after a few days and a guarantee not to starve myself, I was released.

My doctor called to check on me a few days later, and while I was talking to him, I had a major panic attack. I started crying uncontrollably and begging him not to send me back there again. When he asked me where I didn't want to go back to, I couldn't tell him. He stayed on the phone with me for a few minutes and then said he would call me back. When he did, I talked to him in a bizarre, disconnectedly calm voice. He strongly suggested that I get some psychological help and said he would help me find someone to talk to.

All this happened around the same time that Jay and I had decided to start a family, so I was open to the doctor's suggestion. We had been married for three years and everyone was starting to question us about having kids. We knew we didn't want to make the same mistakes our parents had, and so decided we should each get counseling. We wanted to make sure we broke the cycle of abuse before we had a child of our own.

Jay and I both found someone to talk to, and I liked my new therapist. I had no intention of telling him about what happened overseas, but when we talked about the abuse I received from my family of origin, it was clear to him that I was in serious need of help. After a few visits with John, my new psychologist, I found myself agreeing to meet with him several times a week. Six months into therapy, I was pregnant.

Chapter 24
WELCOME CODY

Because I was both consciously and unconsciously rewriting so much of my history, the version of my past that I was willing to share with John was only about my mother. I wanted to make sure that before I had a child, I wasn't like her in any way.

I was pretty certain that what I was sharing with my psychologist didn't match my distress and agitation level. I had been living with the threat of death for five years now, and was used to thinking that I could never tell anyone my whole truth. But John thought that my upset was appropriate. What I had been telling him about my mother convinced him that the abuse I suffered from her seriously interfered with my life, work, marriage, and overall mental health. He used the words "nervous breakdown" and "stress break" a lot during those first two years.

In one of our sessions, I told him about the time my mother grabbed a brush and started brushing my hair furiously. She couldn't get her anger out fast enough and started to hit me over and over again. Her face was contorted with rage as she screamed at me. As I described this to John, I realized I was pantomiming the motion of her hitting me. I stopped, put my hand down in my lap, and calmly waited for his next question. John looked visibly shaken. As usual, I had related this memory with a dead calm. Like all the others, it was no big deal to me. I had survived that and worse. I was clearly in denial.

Once he composed himself, He looked at me with tears in his eyes and said in a crackly voice, "It's a miracle you are alive, you must have a strong will to survive." In a heartbeat, I said, "Yes, I have a golden thread of survival." I didn't know where that came from, but I knew it was true.

I never knew what was going to come out of my mouth during therapy. I had no idea that the level of abuse I survived as a child was worth talking about or bothering with. After all, I was only sharing what happened within the confines of my family. I wasn't telling John about the facility, being prostituted out as a young girl, or that I had gone overseas. I thought that all I was telling him was that I had a mean mother.

Jay was doing well working at a brokerage firm. He was selling risky penny stocks during the Wall Street era of "Greed is good," and was making more money than he ever thought possible. He would call me up and say, "I made $10,000 today!" He was preoccupied with his new life, friends, money, and making big plans for our future. I was genuinely happy for him, and gave him the space to enjoy his personal dreams coming true.

I was terribly sick as soon as I got pregnant. I was diagnosed with Hyperemesis Gravaderum, and vomited all day long for seven months. My doctor demanded I take a leave from work for my whole pregnancy because I was so ill, and dehydration was a constant worry. I still managed to drive to my therapy appointments three times a week because I was desperate to get emotionally better before I became a mom. I was still so disconnected from my body that sometimes I would forget I was pregnant and forgot why I was throwing up. I knew I was pregnant and the baby was growing at a normal rate, but I couldn't quite connect the pregnancy to the illness. This left my therapist John trying to figure out if this was a hormonal response to my pregnancy or if I was surrendering my mental health.

Five months into my pregnancy, my aunt called and told me she was coming to visit from Switzerland. I hadn't seen Edie since I was twelve years old. I was terribly anxious about her staying with us. When she arrived it was as miserable as I had feared. She went from room to room saying, "You don't know how to keep a house. It's clean, but you don't display things in a way that shows off who you are or where you come from." She made me reset the table if it wasn't done to her liking. The strawberries needed to be cut a certain way and the tea needed to be brewed in a certain kind of tea pot. And she complained that I was living beneath my means. I felt terrible and got upset with Jay, telling him he was making me live in a neighborhood full of drug dealers and criminals. I told him my aunt said we needed to buy a house before the baby came.

The next weekend, Jay and I drove Edie around Willow Lake. She had wanted to see the house my parents lived in before my mother moved to the Middle East. On our way home, we passed a house for sale with an open house sign in the driveway.

We pulled over and toured the house. I hated it. I felt an ugly presence lurking behind every door. The house had a cold, almost despairing feel. Jay wasn't impressed either but was not saying much. My aunt looked at us and said, "This is the house you will buy. It has a nice address and that's important." We had no clue what we were doing. We had never even talked about buying a house. We were still in our 20's and home ownership hadn't been on either of our radars. Until my aunt came, we were both content in our duplex in the city. Naively, we agreed with Edie and made an offer on the spot. Three months later, when I was eight months pregnant, we moved into our first home.

As we were getting approved for the loan, I focused on packing up for the move and getting ready for the baby. I bought furniture for our house and the baby. During one of our many ultrasounds the doctor told us we were having a girl. I loved buying little dresses to fill the baby's closet. By the end of my pregnancy, I had been seeing John for over a year. With my

151

mood stabilized and the impending birth, our sessions centered on my day-to-day life. He worked hard to keep my mood stable but light.

Jay and I were both miserable as soon as we moved in. I ran into the former owner of the house one day, and she confessed to me that she and her husband felt really guilty for letting us buy the house, especially when they found out that I was pregnant. She said that the house never had an owner that lasted longer than five years. I confessed to her that from the first day we pulled into the driveway, I felt as if a black cloud hung low over the house. But Jay and I put our feelings about the house behind us, and waited for our bundle of joy to arrive.

We moved in September and my life was a blur until Cody came in early November. As my due date neared, my therapist recognized that I had no idea what to do with a baby. He knew I didn't have any extended family to support me, and that Jay was working long hours. It was becoming more evident every day that I was ill-prepared to be a mom. But I wasn't stressed about it. I never talked about my fears of having a baby. As usual, I was in survival mode.

The baby was due at the end of October, but I didn't go into labor until the middle of the night on November 4th. We were ready. The baby's room was decorated. We had pretty little dresses in the closet and we felt financially secure. I wasn't terribly afraid of giving birth because I was totally disconnected from my body. I never gave a single thought to the fact that I might be triggered by going into another hospital. That is, until we pulled into the parking lot.

I became terribly anxious as we were being admitted. I couldn't handle lying in the bed, and I was afraid of the doctor and nurses. Every time they came in to examine me, I felt myself leave my body. Because my labor wasn't progressing, the doctor decided to break my water. They were wonderful about explaining every decision to both of us, but I wasn't hearing them. When they broke my water I had an intense flashback, and I thought they were killing the baby.

My blood pressure shot through the roof during labor and the baby began showing signs of distress. They decided to give me an epidural and drugs to speed up the labor. I wouldn't cooperate with the epidural. I didn't want someone putting a needle in my spine, and I was upset about having an IV in my arm. I was having terrifying flashbacks and feeling out of control. The whole process was becoming a nightmare.

Fourteen hours later, with a failed epidural, my labor still wasn't progressing. My blood pressure was dangerously high and the baby's distress was now severe. The doctors told Jay they were afraid I was having a stroke and decided to do a C-section. As they wheeled me down the hall I started screaming, thinking they were going to take my baby. Jay stood helplessly by as they rushed me down the hall. He wasn't allowed into the operating room. He said it was the worst feeling in his life, watching me disappear behind the swinging doors.

I was quickly under anesthesia and ten minutes later my son Cody was born. My first memory was of my doctor stroking my head to wake me up. When I opened my eyes, he said, "You have a son." I remember asking before I fell back asleep, "Did you say I had a son?" For more than half my pregnancy we had been expecting a daughter.

Cody had been born with the umbilical cord wrapped twice around his neck and was blue. He had aspirated amniotic fluid into his lungs. He had an Apgar score of one on a scale of one to ten. He was a very sick, but very big baby; 8 lbs, 11 oz and 21 ½ inches long. Because he was so sick, Cody ended up in the newborn ICU for seven days.

A few hours after he was born, I began to hemorrhage. The nurses came into my room, woke me out of a drugged and weakened state, and told me to call Jay to tell him I needed a transfusion. I will never forget the fear in their faces as they tried to stop the bleeding. Neither Jay nor I understood how dangerous my hemorrhaging was.

Both Cody and I were very sick and fragile that first week. Although several people came to see me and the baby, I had no memory of them. My visits were limited to five minutes and they could only see Cody from a distance at the NICU. Jay was allowed to hold and bathe him, and bonded with him immediately. He was thrilled to return all the little girl clothes and buy boy things. He even bought Cody a little suit, so he could look like his stock broker daddy.

The only person I have a memory of coming to see me in the hospital was my therapist, John. He told me he had seen the baby and how he was proud of me. I told him that we named the baby Cody but that his middle name was John in honor of him, and in gratitude for all that he had done to help me. He was surprised and touched by this, and gently held my hand until I fell back asleep.

I was only allowed to go to the nursery one time during those first seven days. The nurses wheeled me down to Cody, but I was too weak to hold him. All I could do was look at him for a few moments sleeping in his Lucite box. I felt terribly sad that I didn't get to hold my baby, but I was too sick to make a fuss and I knew I needed to get back to bed.

It wasn't until seven days after I gave birth and was feeling better that the nurses brought Cody into my room. As they carried my little bundle of baby into the room, I felt all my fears and guilt for not being able to care for him until then, melt away. I eagerly held out my arms and held him for the first time.

From my journal~

To Cody: I had to catch my breath when I first looked into those beautiful eyes. I fell instantly in love. A love I knew I never felt before. It welled up from deep inside me and spilled from my eyes.

Cody is now 28 years old. Every year on his birthday I tell him the story of that moment when I first looked into his beautiful bright blue eyes, patted his mass of strawberry blond hair and said, "I'm your mommy and I will love and protect you forever." I couldn't have known that the birth of my son stirred excitement and planning halfway across the world, in the desert country that I was trying so hard to forget.

Chapter 25
SETTING BOUNDARIES

The day before Cody was born my brother Adam called. I hadn't heard from him since my wedding four years earlier, so I was surprised. The first words out of his mouth were that he heard I wasn't going to name my baby after our father. I told him that was true, and pointed out that he hadn't named his two children after our father either. "That's not the point," he said defensively, "It's your responsibility to do what's expected for the family." Adam said he had spoken with our mother and she told him that she'd received a letter from us outlining a set of rules if she wanted to meet our baby. I said yes, I had written a letter setting some boundaries. I also told him I was seeing a therapist, and was working hard to find out a way to stop being manipulated by our mother.

Adam became enraged. Yelling and swearing at me, he said, "You have no right to ever interfere with the rights of the family. Mother should have access to her grandchild whenever she wants. How dare you let any therapist interfere with our family?" I was stunned. I didn't know how to handle his tirade, so I just sat listening while he screamed. When he was finished hurling insults and threats, he hung up on me. We didn't speak to each other again for five years.

My mother had come to town three months before Cody was born. Following John's suggestion, I asked if she would like to come to therapy with me and she said, "Yes." I knew she would agree. By this time I understood that she was a narcissist, and would never pass up a chance to be center stage and complain about all the ways I had ruined her life. Even though John was always supportive and compassionate, I could tell that sometimes he wondered if I was embellishing my stories a little. I let her do all the talking when we met with John. I knew she wouldn't disappoint me. Her mental illness would be obvious as soon as we sat down. John was clearly unnerved by my mother's diatribe. When he and I met for a session the next day, he said that she was much crueler than I had given her credit for, or than he had imagined. He offered to help me compose a letter to her before she came back to meet the baby.

With his help, I wrote a letter to my mother outlining some clear boundaries. I wrote that she could come and see the new baby at a time that was convenient for both me and Jay. She was not welcome to stay in our house and that if she couldn't stay with friends, we would give her a list of hotels in the area. I also said that she needed to rent a car instead of using mine, and finally, that if she started to verbally abuse me, she would be asked to leave our house immediately. It took a tremendous amount of courage for me to write that letter. In fact, if John hadn't walked with me to the mailbox so I wouldn't change my mind, I might not have been able to send it.

I knew how she would react and so her call didn't surprise me. She was livid. She hurled insults at me, saying how evil and cruel I was, and that she hated me. She said that she had spoken to her attorney and was told she had a right to see her only grandson. She blamed my therapist for interfering in family business and told me she was going to sue him. Just like Adam, when she finished ranting, she hung up on me. During the phone call, I had managed to interject, "If you don't want to follow the rules then you can't meet Cody." She responded the same way every time I made a boundary, "We'll just see about that."

I was steadfast in my resolve to follow through with the boundaries that John helped me lay out. It was the first time I had someone in my corner that wasn't afraid of my family. John had no fear of my mother. I felt he wanted to protect me from her. I never wavered from the script he taught me. I stood my ground when she challenged the terms of her visit, no matter how verbally abusive she got on the phone. My mother finally acquiesced. She said she would stay with a friend and would come and meet the baby at a time that Jay and I chose.

Having a new baby in the house was exhausting. Anticipating my mother's arrival, I became afraid for my son's safety. I could feel myself losing confidence in my ability to stay calm. John met with Jay and asked him to intervene on my behalf as soon as my mother broke any of the rules we had spelled out for her. He happily agreed.

She came to visit when Cody was two months old. We all expected that with the conditions I outlined in the letter and her raging phone calls in response to it, that she was likely to come at me full force.

That first evening proved to be as disastrous as we expected. Because Cody was asleep, she was only allowed to look at him in his crib. This instantly made her angry. She was furious that I wasn't willing to wake him up. Then she ranted about not being welcome to stay in our house or take one of our cars. She yelled that we had no right to set any parameters around her visit. Within five minutes of walking into our house, she had violated the entire list of conditions that were laid out in my letter.

Trying to calm her erupting rage, Jay asked her to sit down for a cup of tea. I was already checking out mentally. I knew she was just getting started, and I could feel my own rage beginning to bubble up.

I assumed that Jay was no match for her. He didn't have the experience I did with her manipulation, so I was steeling myself for the fight. As soon as I sat down across from her, my mother looked at me and said, "You are a disgusting, evil person." That's all it took. Jay and I had been together for six years, but I had never seen him get clearly angry at another person until then.

"That's it!" he said loudly, "I'm calling you a cab and you're leaving right now." My mother and I were both shocked into silence as we watched him phone for a taxi. I don't think my mother had ever been talked to like that by anyone in her life other than her children. I watched the stunned expression on her face as Jay escorted her down the stairs to wait by the door for the taxi. As he stood there with her, he said, "If you're willing to follow our rules, you can come back tomorrow and try it again." I didn't say a word. I was stunned. This was the first time anyone had ever dared to intervene between me and any of my family members.

After the cab left, Jay wouldn't talk about it. He went straight to bed. I don't think he knew how to deal with what had happened either. Not only had he witnessed how cruel my mother could be, but I'm sure he never thought he would ever have to throw his mother-in-law out of his house. As I sat on the couch after Jay went to bed, I wondered what the next day would bring. I had never known my mother to back down. She would regroup for another attack, with Jay as her newest enemy.

When she came back to meet Cody the following day, I made sure that either Jay or one my friends was in the room with us when she was with the baby. That was one of my therapist's rules. He didn't want me to be alone with her. I watched my mother love and speak kindly to Cody. I was glad that she was able to treat him with tenderness and feel proud of her grandson, but I never let my guard down. I knew she was a snake in the grass ready to strike. I knew that she was still angry at Jay and there would be consequences; but it warmed my heart to know that for the moment, she was showing loving kindness to an innocent child, giving Cody something she had always denied me.

Every time my mother visited we had to reiterate the ground rules. When Cody was about a year old, she started calling to tell me that as his grandmother, she had every right to take him to the Middle East and introduce him to everyone there. She was adamant that Cody follow in his grandfather's footsteps. It was important that my father's legacy live on. I would become hysterical and scream back at her, "You will never get your hands on my child, and he will never step foot in that country."

I didn't trust anyone with Cody. After those calls, I was seeing danger and threats to my son everywhere. About the same time, Jay got a call from my mother's attorney and was summoned to a meeting at his office. He came home visibly shaken, but wouldn't tell me what they talked about. Jay said he had also met someone who told him that they had known my father. I started to see handlers everywhere, and I became even more over-protective of Cody.

It was more and more difficult to keep the truth of what had happened to me overseas, from my therapist John. He was asking me questions during therapy about my life right before I met Jay, and I felt really uneasy. I had been back from the Middle East for eight years by this time, but I still heard the hissed threat in my ear to never talk about what happened. And with my mother's demands to take Cody overseas increasing, I was afraid that I wouldn't be able to keep the secrets from John much longer. Something had to give.

I convinced myself that it was okay to tell John about my childhood, but nothing about going overseas. I had survived, and I had to keep surviving until Cody, and any of my future children, were grown. So I started cancelling my appointments with him and eventually stopped going to therapy all together. I offered John no explanations for wanting to stop our sessions. I went from three days a week to nothing. I felt miserable and empty inside, but I was also becoming more adept at repressing the past.

It was getting easier to forget who I was and where I had been, as I focused on both my son and a new job working in a health club.

Chapter 26
WELCOME ARIA

In the financial world, Monday, October 19, 1987 is known as Black Monday, the largest one-day stock market crash in history. I vividly remember Jay coming home from work that night. He slumped on the couch and loosened his tie, looking shaken and defeated. He looked down at the floor and said, "I lost all my clients' money today."

I sat across the room, listening to him recount what happened that day. I asked him if we were going to be okay, and he said, "Yes." I knew we had money in savings, but I didn't know how long that would carry us through.

Jay had made a lot of money and very fast before he was 30 years old. We were both young and naïve, and had no idea how to manage that amount of money. The prevailing message in Jay's industry was that the money would never stop, "Keep selling stock and stay motivated by buying bigger houses and better cars. Look the part, so you can live the part." Neither one of us had any adult role models to advise us, so we floundered when his six figure income dropped to less than $10,000 the following year.

Cody was about a year old when the market crashed. I was working in a large health club in the evenings and helping a friend open a new health club near our house. Jay and I worked opposite shifts. During the day he tried to piece his business back together. As soon as he got home in the evening I would pass him the baby and go to work myself. We rarely saw each other and ignored the elephant in the room; our financial life was slowly unraveling.

As the drama of Black Monday subsided, we both focused on earning money and raising our child. I was still dealing with occasional phone calls from Arik, saying, "Just calling to say hi," but I focused on enjoying Cody and working. My mother's visits had increased to twice a year. She would split her time between my siblings and our house. Every time she came, we argued as she pushed the boundaries. I was torn when she visited, not only by her verbal abuse and threats about taking my baby overseas, but also because she was genuinely sweet and loving with Cody. Jay was estranged from his family, and we were both caught up in the notion that our children should know one of their grandparents.

When Cody was three years old, my mother brought a painting with her. As she slowly unwrapped it, she told me that Daniel had painted me a scene from the river. The room seemed to sway under my feet. I felt my stomach drop, and then waves of nausea began to sweep over me. I didn't think I would ever hear Daniel's name, or have to think about that river, again. I had almost convinced myself that what happened in the tunnel was just a scene in a very bad dream I had.

I looked at the painting, a watercolor of children playing along the banks of the river. I flashed back to the day that Daniel and I stood by that river, before he walked me into the dusty town and into the tunnel, the day he told me what my assignment was and then threatened my life.

My mother said that Daniel wanted me to know that he had painted this for his "Little One." He told my mother to suggest that it hang in a place of honor in my house, so that I'd always be reminded of that beautiful day by the river.

I was in a fearful, trance-like state as I let my mother help me hang the painting over our living room couch. Jay didn't care for it. He didn't like the muted colors or the scene, but I insisted on keeping it on the wall. In fact, that painting hung in every home we lived in for the next twenty-seven years, standing guard over me, an ever-present reminder that they could end my life at any time.

Besides the occasional calls from Arik, I had received a couple of other calls that kept me on edge. My mother's lawyer called one day and told me that I was acting irresponsibly, and that I should let my mother travel with Cody. I even got a call from the rabbi that took me on the field trip to the State Hospital after my father died. I was hyper-vigilant with our son as he grew, making sure he was always with either Jay, or very close friends.

Cody was now in pre-school full time, Jay was working hard to rebuild his clientele, and I was working at a health club. I knew in the back of my mind that we were in a steady financial decline, but I trusted Jay when he reassured me that we were okay. I thought that the money I was bringing in from work and our savings was still enough of a cushion, but any unexpected expense would be disastrous. At the same time, Jay and I decided it was time for our family to grow.

After I delivered Cody, I'd asked the doctor what the chances were that I would be as sick with a second pregnancy as I was with the first. He told me my chances were 50/50. What I focused on was that there was a 50% chance I wouldn't be sick again, and I wanted to try for another child. When we got the joyful news that I was pregnant in January of 1991, I began throwing up continuously.

Once again I had developed Hyperemesis Gravaderum. This time I was a lot sicker, not just unable to work but confined to bed. I was admitted to the hospital for dehydration for days at a time, and was too sick to take care of Cody. Fortunately, my old roommate Grace lived nearby, and was a stay-at-home mom. She offered to take care of Cody during the day while Jay worked. I knew Cody was safe with her.

As I lay sick in bed, day after day, not working, I worried that we were headed for financial ruin, but Jay kept assuring me that we were okay. He was exhausted, trying to sell stock at a time when no one was investing in the market, being a single parent in the evenings, and taking care of me. He started missing work as the stress of his everyday life weighed heavy on his shoulders.

I started feeling better around the 8th month of my pregnancy. I had numerous ultrasounds. An enhanced version at the hospital left us no doubt that we were having a baby girl. After all the difficulty I had delivering Cody, we planned a C-section. On August 21st, with Jay in the room watching, our healthy and beautiful daughter Aria arrived.

The doctor decided on the spot to tie my tubes. He said I couldn't risk another pregnancy. I didn't care; I gave him permission to do whatever was needed. I was just thrilled to see Jay holding our healthy new baby in his arms. We were now a family of four, and I vowed to do whatever it took to protect my two children. I was afraid that Aria's dark hair and dark complexion would make her a prize to the same people overseas who had threatened me.

Chapter 27
THE APARTMENT

I had no idea when Aria was born that our finances were beyond repair, or that we were months away from losing our house. Our foreclosure was already in process, and we were thousands of dollars in debt. Jay's business was non-existent, and I hadn't been able to work during my pregnancy. I found out how dire our situation was, the day someone knocked on our door to repossess the car.

I confronted Jay when he came home that day, and he told me the truth. He had been hiding it all from me. When I fell sick during my pregnancy, and turned over all the responsibility for our finances to him, he got overwhelmed. Between worrying about my precarious health, his single parenting duties, and watching his business disappear, he found he couldn't manage. I was livid that he hadn't shared how much trouble we were in earlier, and I refused to listen to his explanations. I felt betrayed by the person I had most trusted to keep us safe, and told him that I would never be able to trust him again. A few days later, we met with an attorney who advised us to file for bankruptcy.

This happened in an era when filing for bankruptcy carried a heavy stigma. Our lawyer told us that we would never be able to buy a car, own a house, or even open a checking account again. The shame heaped upon us was an enormous burden for Jay to bear. He had pulled himself out of the gutter, fulfilled his dream of making money, was supporting a family that he loved, and was living his idea of the good life. And now, it was all gone. Not only was it gone, but he felt ostracized by the society he so desperately wanted to be a part of.

I didn't share what was happening right away with any of my friends, because I was embarrassed. None of them had gone through anything like this and I felt ashamed. I was angry at Jay. I was embarrassed that we were losing our house, and our marriage was falling apart with every passing day. Jay and I didn't know how to communicate with each other and couldn't work well together to figure out what our next steps should be. The angrier I got, the more he spiraled into feeling like a failure as a husband, father, and provider. He was devastated and heartbroken. I felt betrayed and lied to. Along with losing our home, we were losing any semblance of a relationship.

Two weeks before we went to court, I finally confided in my friends. None of them made me feel that we had failed. They tried to gently tell me that Jay was trying to protect me by not telling me the truth, but I was too angry to hear any of it. I didn't think they were taking sides because I knew they had a broader perspective, but I simply couldn't hear them. I had put Jay in the same category as my abusers, and nothing was going to make me forgive him. I couldn't see that our finances had slowly deteriorated over time. Our communication had been stunted from the beginning of our relationship, and now we couldn't find a way to work through this crisis.

I knew we had to move. I didn't have a clue about how to find an apartment without money to cover rent. It never occurred to me to ask for assistance, but when a friend volunteered to help me, I found Section 8 housing in the district where I wanted Cody to start school. She helped me get emergency funding for the first few months rent, and took me to the welfare office where I got food stamps to tide us over until I could find a job. I sat in a daze during those interviews. They deemed us destitute enough to be given a monthly stipend. I remember sitting in the waiting room thinking, how did I go from making ends meet on my own, to making a good income with my husband, to being homeless in just five years? Losing the material stuff didn't matter to me. What mattered was how I had lost control of my life.

The day before we moved out of the house, I sat on the living room floor and for the first time sobbed over all those losses. I couldn't stop blaming Jay, and didn't know how to forgive him. I didn't have any tools to deal with relationship strife, so I went to the place I felt the most comfortable, to my ability to detach. I held myself together but my detachment from Jay plus his own feelings of failure had him retreating further and further into himself. He was spiraling into a deep depression.

Moving day was a flurry of activity. One of my friends came to take the kids overnight, another friend put herself in charge of moving the cats, and Jay and his friends handled the furniture and boxes. I left it up to Jay to sell everything that wouldn't fit into the small apartment. We needed cash for food and getting settled.

After all the furniture was gone, I stood in the empty living room, feeling lonely and scared. I knew I would survive somehow and I would make sure my kids were okay, but I heard myself saying, "Just make it through the next ten minutes." That was the mantra I used so many times when I was being abused as a child. I knew I wasn't being abused now, but to get through this I needed every last coping skill.

I was grateful we had enough people in our lives to make sure my kids were well cared for. Aria was only six months old, but Cody was old enough to know he wasn't going home to his same house. Our friends turned our move into an adventure for him. Jay and I knew at some unspoken level that our marriage was in deep trouble.

I felt in a trance the first time I walked up the shabby stairs to the apartment. The dank and moldy smell in the hallway, the sounds from the other tenants, and the gloomy surroundings were overwhelming. The rooms were packed wall-to-wall with boxes and furniture. I couldn't find the cats for a while and got very upset. Then I began to obsess about where to put their litter boxes in this tiny place. Jay and his friends had put together the crib for Aria, and mine and Cody's beds. When everyone had left, I sat down in a chair and began to cry. I asked Jay what we were going to do. He walked over to me and said, "I can't handle this, I need to leave." He turned around and walked out the door. I was left alone with all the boxes to unpack and the furniture to put in place before the kids came to their new home the next morning.

Watching Jay walk out the door only solidified my belief that he was just like all the other people in my life who had hurt me. He had abandoned me, walked away, turned around and left. It was like watching Arik walk away from me in the market square. I thought I might never see Jay again, but I had been too tired and angry to say anything to stop him. Neither of us knew he was experiencing the beginning of a dangerous manic episode. We had never really talked about his bipolar condition. He took his meds and that was that. The next day, we decided to separate.

Jay moved in with his brother, so he had the support he needed to figure out how to rebuild his life. He struggled with his mental health but found the right therapist, and with medication combinations, he eventually stabilized. He decided he had enough with sales and pursued a profession in construction, eventually becoming a commercial cabinet maker.

I still felt incredibly hurt and angry towards him, but we both felt strongly that he needed to see our kids every day. He was a good father and they loved him. He and Cody had a strong relationship and even though Aria was still a baby, she lit up whenever her dad was around. He cared for the kids while I worked in the evening, and they had a solid bedtime routine of books and songs. Neither one of us wanted that to change. So again, I found a job working evenings so Jay could care for the kids until I got home. The only conversations we had were centered on the kids.

I was getting used to living apart from Jay. I had totally detached myself from thinking about him as anything but the kids' father. We didn't consider marriage counseling. I still blamed Jay for our misfortune, and took no responsibility for any part I may have had in it. We had a good routine and no issues when it came to co-parenting. The only time we were contentious was the day I said in passing, that I was thinking about taking the kids and moving out of the state to start over. He blew up saying, "I will never allow you to move my kids anywhere." I realized how much he loved Cody and Aria, and knew that they loved him, so I never considered moving away from him again.

I tried to make the apartment as homey as I could for the kids. There was no place for Cody to play outside and I was worried about the influence of some of the other kids in the complex. It was obvious to me that there were drugs being sold on the patch of grass on the side of the apartment, and there was an eerie pall, a weird silence, in the parking lot. All I wanted was for the kids to feel safe. I knew how precious that feeling was, and I didn't want them to go to bed or to wake up being afraid. All this fueled my anger and frustration toward Jay. It went from an achy burn to a full flame. At the same time, I was hugely depressed and wanted to just curl up in bed and forget everything.

Only a few days after we moved into the apartment, I found a letter in the mailbox. I hadn't filled out a change of address card yet, so I thought it was really odd that we had mail. The only people who knew my address were the welfare department and my employer. It was a plain white envelope with no return address, but I opened it anyway. The only thing inside it was a newspaper clipping.

It was article about a woman who was killed in a car accident a few months before. As I read her name, I felt an icy chill run down my spine. I began to panic as I realized that this same woman had been my father's hospice nurse. They were very close the last year of his life and had become each other's confidant. I hadn't spoken to her in close to fourteen years. But, I knew this article was a not-so-subtle reminder that no matter where I moved, my handlers would always be able to find me. My right ear stung with the hiss of the threat delivered to me eleven years earlier, just before I was dropped off at a small airport overseas.

When I opened the letter I was standing by the couch where Aria was sleeping. My stomach tied itself in knots. My daughter's looks were identical to mine. I had been so focused on Cody being in danger with my mother threatening to take him overseas. What if the horrific life that had been laid out for me in that tunnel years before, became Aria's fate?

In that moment, I decided I was the only one who could truly protect my children and that I would, at any cost. My fear turned into anger and determination. I knew I had to push aside my depression, listen to my intuition, and make some choices. I knew the kids weren't in imminent danger, but that newspaper clipping galvanized me into action.

I decided I needed to finish my degree, get a good paying job, and never let my emotions get in the way of keeping a vigilant eye out for danger. I also knew I had to get us out of that apartment building. That envelope was just one more thing making me feel unsafe there, and Cody, now five years old, had recently come home telling me he learned all about sex from the girl who lived downstairs.

The next morning I headed to the library for a list of colleges and started calling to find the right program for me. I enrolled in an accelerated degree program that I could attend once a week. I was promoted to manager at the daycare center where I worked, and started to take control of my life. All of this happened within a week of my receiving the newspaper clipping. I was becoming obsessed with providing safety for my children and any feelings that got in the way of that, I beat down.

In the nine months after losing our house, I had separated from Jay, gone on welfare, moved into a dangerous neighborhood, gotten a full time job, and enrolled in college. Now, I found us a new place to live.

It was in a quiet neighborhood in Willow Lake with a fenced-in back yard where the kids could play safely. Jay and I were starting to talk a little more. He was supportive of my going back to school and helped us pack and move. I knew that wherever our relationship went, I would never let anyone else control my finances again. He and I agreed after lots of talking, that we were ready to try marriage counseling to see if we could repair our relationship. A year later we reconciled, committed to being open and truthful with each other. I agreed, but I wasn't entirely truthful. Jay still had no idea what had happened to me overseas and the threats that I was living under. I thought I still needed to protect him and our kids by staying silent. I was never going to put any of them in danger.

Chapter 28
LIVING A NORMAL FAMILY LIFE

Once we moved from the apartment it became my life's mission to keep a protective bubble around my family. At some level I knew I was being unreasonable and overprotective with my children. When I got together with other parents, I could clearly see that they loved and wanted to protect their kids as much as I did, but they weren't constantly looking around corners for the same threats that I felt I needed to shield Cody and Aria from. The only time I could relax was when they were sound asleep.

I attended Early Childhood Family Education classes and made sure that the kids had plenty of play dates. I worked in daycare so they were near me as I kept a sharp eye out for danger. At first I talked with other parents so I could get some ideas on how they kept their kids safe, but I quickly saw that they didn't share my fears. They had the "normal" fears most parents had for their children. They child-proofed their houses and taught their kids not to touch hot stoves, to look both ways before crossing the street, and to not go off with strangers. No one could relate to my fear that my two children might be taken off to another country at any moment. At first I thought, "What's wrong with these parents?" Then I realized that I was the one that was going overboard. I sat back and watched how other parents interacted with their kids. I was great at reading social cues and quickly learned how typical parents saw the world, so I wouldn't smother Cody and Aria with my own fears.

We were invited to all the Mommy and Me events, and I desperately wanted to fit in, so I kept my fears tucked inside and stopped questioning the other parents. I was an introvert by nature so preferred to be at home where I could control my surroundings, but I also didn't want to isolate my children.

Four years after we filed bankruptcy, I graduated with honors with a degree in Business Management. I was extremely proud of myself for staying the course and not letting anything interfere with reaching my goal. Along with school, I was working full time and traveling back and forth to visit my sister who had been diagnosed with a serious illness. I was being pulled in many directions. Phone calls from overseas still came, with the simple message, "Nothing has changed." I would hang up on the caller, and found a way to shake off the threat without pausing to even think about them.

I didn't realize it at the time, but I was functioning so well because I dissociated from any stress or fear I experienced. My pattern was to push feelings aside and keep moving. I imposed very rigid rules on my thoughts and behavior. If I felt tired, I'd berate myself, calling myself stupid and lazy. In very unkind ways, I reminded myself that failure was never an option.

I told myself not to trust anyone, and to never ask for help. I needed to do everything on my own. I told myself to sleep lightly, and never fall sleep before the kids did. I paid rapt attention to the world around me, keeping a vigilant eye on what was happening in the Middle East. I had rules around what I could and couldn't eat, how and where to travel, the best time to go shopping, and every imaginable day-to-day activity. I didn't realize at the time that my behavior was rooted in my past trauma. I had convinced myself that I had done a great job of repressing my past and handling the stress of the veiled but continual threats.

I could put on a great public face. I was outgoing in small group settings where I felt at ease and in control, but I was extremely uncomfortable in larger groups. I'm sure I came across as shy and aloof. The truth was that in a crowd of people, I had a hard time reading all the social cues and non-verbal communication. I'd get agitated at losing control over my surroundings. Going into a crowded room I would always check for exits, so I could quickly leave if I needed to. I was always trying to discern who was dangerous from who was safe, so functioning in large group settings was exhausting.

I found that same ability to read people was a great career asset. I excelled as a personal trainer, sales person, and recruiter. Professionally, I turned my quirks into stable employment, but emotionally, I was exhausted and lonely, filled with fear and dread. Still, I felt enormous happiness and pride when it came to my children. Even though I felt the need to protect them, I immersed myself in watching Cody and Aria, and relishing their childhood innocence.

Aria started kindergarten the same year I graduated from college. She had been by my side for five years, but I felt comfortable knowing that she would be at the same elementary school as Cody. As soon as she started school I felt everything slowing down. With my degree, I got a full time job recruiting for a senior companionship company, and the kids were both in school all day. For the first time in my life, at 36, I had some down time. I'd always managed to keep myself busy and moving, and now I was faced with stillness.

I began to experience almost debilitating mental anguish and pain. All the feelings that I had suppressed and denied were beginning to seep into the spaces in my everyday life. Feelings of helplessness, hopelessness, and dread kept surfacing. I had to find a way to quash them. I had no way to name what was happening to me. In deep denial, I recognized that the only thing that had changed was that I wasn't constantly moving, so I found ways to push myself again. I started exercising excessively, and for the next twelve years would often work out to the point of injury. I had disconnected from my body long ago, so I exercised my way to countless pulled or torn muscles.

Jay and I were back on our feet financially, so six years after we filed for bankruptcy we began to look at homes. We found the perfect house for us. We were ecstatic and the kids seemed comfortable, well adjusted, and happy.

My repressed past and the effects of my trauma were muted, but were ever-present. They were a constant undertow in the flow of my relationships, the way I ran my life, my work, and my health. The toll it took on my physical health led to numerous hospitalizations, fibromyalgia, high blood pressure, low blood pressure, inner ear disturbances, and more.

I had no idea that I was suffering from Posttraumatic Stress Disorder. It had been fifteen years since I'd come home from overseas. I'd repressed the memories I needed to, I'd managed to push away the threats that came in letters or phone calls by telling myself that they just didn't happen, and I had an amazing ability to focus on only what was right in front of me. It wasn't that I was living in the moment; I was just continually on the move.

"Just keep moving" was my mantra, but I instinctively knew I needed something to connect with, to anchor me. I felt myself slipping away. I heard of meditation as a way to sit still and gather yourself and your thoughts, so I started reading everything I could find on meditation, Buddhism, yoga, and finding inner peace. I skipped the psychological self help books. I needed something to nourish my spirit. I felt as if my soul was missing or shattered, and I knew I wanted to connect with the part of me that had survived, my spirit. I was convinced that my spirit was what had kept me alive all those years. What I didn't realize was that I also needed help with the trauma I had suffered, because it was eating away at my health.

I sought out a path of peace within myself. I believed I was beginning to look at the world differently, but during the first years of my practice, I was simply dissociating from my pain, ignoring the trauma, and withdrawing from the reality of my past. I was able to live in the moment because that was my primary survival technique. I didn't understand what it meant to be truly present or to connect with the perfection of a moment. I had the concept of what I was trying to learn turned upside down, so I continued to tie myself into a tighter knot. It was only years later, that what I had learned began to feed a very deep part of me. The knowledge patiently waited. Over time, I learned how to incorporate those teachings, and several times had the gift of clarity and connectedness. But first, I had to endure years of unexplained physical illness.

When I was diagnosed with fibromyalgia, I was prescribed heavy doses of propoxyphene. I hated the way the drug made me feel and often complained to my doctor. On one such phone call, he said, "You need to just learn to live with the discomfort and take the meds." I was livid. I wasn't willing to live my life in pain and take a medication with nasty side effects. I researched other ways to manage pain, and sought the help of an acupuncturist. I felt an instant connection to Simon. He truly changed the course of my life and became one my most important teachers and mentors. Simon is still an integral part of my healthcare eleven years later.

When I first started seeing him, I not only complained of fibromyalgia, but told him I suffered from constant stomach aches, headaches, and terrible fatigue. I kept telling him that none of this could be emotional because my life was stable. Compared to what it had looked like earlier, my life *was* stable. I had repressed my memories, was able to forget a threat the moment I read it or hung up the phone, and continued to practice expert denial. The more Simon asked about any emotional wounding, the more I told myself that was impossible. I told him that I had seen a therapist seventeen years earlier and that all my issues had been resolved. I truly believed what I was saying. Simon patiently continued to plant the seed that I might be suffering from something emotional as well as physical, and that perhaps he could help me find someone to talk to when I was ready.

This exchange went on for the first five years he treated me. Now, we can laugh about the day that I finally started therapy again. I tease him that he went out and celebrated with huge sighs of relief and lots of champagne. I give Simon full credit for saving my life, and will always be grateful for his grace, patience, and commitment to me.

Simon's calm demeanor and deep commitment to my health and well being gave me the sense of safety that I desperately needed. I found I could finally let my guard down. As safe as I felt at his office, whenever he tried to leave the room so I could relax during treatment, I would hear myself asking, "Are they coming for me?" He would always reassure me before he closed the door that I was safe and no one was coming. There were times that I would ask him to take the "snakes" off my stomach, or ask if I was bleeding from my arms. I could hear myself asking those questions, but refused to believe that the words were actually coming out of my mouth. I kept telling myself that his treatments were putting me in a really altered state, but somewhere deep inside; I knew that the questions I was asking were coming from a profoundly tangled truth.

I would often leave acupuncture feeling dazed, confused, and unnerved, thinking I was going crazy. But I kept going back because my wise self knew how critical and timely Simon's help was. Not only was I unconsciously yearning to tell the truth of my past, but I found I was actually feeling better physically.

Simon was the first person I ever told about my nightmares. I was terrified to go to sleep at night, so he loaned me what he called his "dream warriors" to keep me safe. Sometimes after a treatment I would get overwhelmed and start to cry. Without saying a word, he would gently put his arms around me and wait until my tears stopped, and I was able to drive home. He made himself available after hours if I needed to check in. He was always there with patience and respect, all the while encouraging me to seek psychological help.

I kept chalking up these experiences as my reaction to acupuncture, and ignoring that my emotional unraveling was real or serious. I kept telling myself to work hard during the day, exercise at night, and be the perfect mom, and then everything would be okay. Even though Simon explained to me time and time again, that I needed more help than he could provide, I kept my perfect denial intact. I was an expert at compartmentalizing the pieces of my life, or at least I thought I was. At the same time, I couldn't deny that I was becoming increasingly agitated and sensitive at work, and less adept at deflecting the constant stress I was heaping on myself. My memories continued to erupt to the surface.

I handled this by withdrawing. I stopped doing things socially and found every excuse to be by myself. I deluded myself into thinking I was becoming more introspective and calm. I was "letting go" and "just being" while I delved deeper into the Zen of yoga. I was doing everything I could both consciously and unconsciously to keep living in denial, but my façade was starting to crumble. The impenetrable walls that protected me from myself were losing their strength. I felt like I was slowly going crazy.

Everything exploded on October 9, 2007 when Aria was hit by a van going 30 miles an hour as she crossed the street. I was at work when I answered my phone and glanced down at the caller ID to see "Willow Lake Police Department." I stood up, blinked, heard a keening sound, and felt something crack in my brain. It felt as if a mirror had shattered into a million pieces, and was raining down inside my head. And then, for mere seconds, I experienced the most vivid and intense flashback of my life. I saw a girl sitting in a small airport; battered, bruised, and alone.

Chapter 29
THINGS WILL NEVER BE THE SAME AGAIN

Aria and I were having a very difficult time communicating with each other at the beginning of her junior year of high school. She was strong-willed and stubborn, a typical 16-year-old. Rebelling by staying up too late, not doing her homework, and refusing to get up in time for school in the mornings, she was continuously missing the bus.

Those mornings I had two choices. I could start off with an argument and drive Aria to school, making me five to ten minutes late for work, or nag her every couple of minutes to get out of bed. Our days almost always began with conflict, and it was only October.

The morning of October 9th, I tried several times to get Aria out of bed but finally gave up because I had to leave for work. The last time I tried to rouse her she snarled, "I'm up, *GO* to work." I left in a huff, got to work and organized my office to begin my day. About 45 minutes later, Aria called me on my work phone and told me she had missed both a ride from her friend, and the bus. I was furious. I told her, "Get your ass out of bed and walk to school." She was angry at me and I was angry at her, another typical start to both our mornings.

It was my habit to keep my cell phone in my purse when I was at work. The kids knew to call my work phone if they wanted to talk. But that morning, something told me to look at my phone about 10 or 15 minutes after I hung up with Aria. I noticed there was a voice message and decided to listen to it. On the phone was a man's shaky voice saying, "Your daughter has been hit by a car, please call the police." At the same time that I was listening to the message, my desk phone rang, and I glanced down to see that it was the police calling me. They told me that Aria had been hit by a car and they were going to patch me through to the ambulance. I could hear the siren in the background as the paramedic told me, "Your daughter was hit by a van. We're taking her to the hospital. You need to get there as soon as you can." The paramedic asked me if I wanted to talk to her and put the phone up to Aria's ear. I heard them say to her, "Your mom is on the phone." My rebellious teenager, who just an hour earlier was beyond infuriated with me, said in a scared, little voice, that I will never forget, "Mommy, I'm hurt!" I said, "You will be okay, just hold on. I'm on my way to the hospital."

I hung up the phone and heard a noise that I assumed came out of me, because several co-workers and my boss came running into my office. I don't remember the exact noise, but I do remember the feeling of glass breaking in my head, and then an intense vision of a battered and bruised girl sitting at an airport. The vision left as quickly as it came. I heard myself saying to my co-workers that Aria was just hit by a car and I need to get to the hospital. One of them took me by the hand and led me to her car. As we were driving toward the freeway, we passed the spot where Aria had been hit. There were still four police cars, a van, and several people standing on the curb talking to the police. It didn't register with me at the time, that the van I saw at the accident scene was the vehicle that hit Aria, or how severe her injuries must have been. I didn't connect that they were taking her to a trauma hospital instead of the nearest one, less than two miles away. I remember turning my head and looking behind me, saying in a voice that sounded otherworldly, "That's where it must have happened."

I called both Jay and Cody on the way to the hospital, telling them to meet me there immediately because Aria was hit by a car, but I didn't have any other information. I don't remember either of their reactions. The only thing I could focus on was getting to my daughter. With the car barely coming to a stop at the emergency room, I leapt out and ran inside. A police officer was waiting for me and led me to her right away. I could hear him talking to me as we were rushing down the hall, but the only words that really registered were when he said, "She is one lucky girl." I don't remember what he looked like, or anything else he said, but I remember those words as clearly today as I did back then.

When they brought me into Aria's room, I couldn't believe my eyes. Lying on a gurney, with her head and neck immobilized was my little girl. They were cutting off her clothes and asking her questions. She was unrecognizable. Her whole face was bloody and swollen. I could immediately see that her teeth were missing. It was clear that she had fallen flat on her face. I rushed over to her, held her hand as tight as I could, and listened to the doctors and nurses talking to her. At a one point, one of the doctors asked Aria if she had any questions. Through swollen lips and a mouth missing teeth, she very quietly asked, "Will I still be pretty?" The doctor said, "Yes" and assured her that she was beautiful. That very innocent and age-appropriate question from my 16-year-old was music to my ears. My Aria was still in there, under all that swelling, and I knew in that moment that she was going to be okay.

Jay and Cody arrived within half an hour of me. The emergency room team let all three of us stay with Aria even though someone had mentioned that the rules were that only one person could be with her at a time. Maybe it was clear to the doctors and nurses that all of us needed to be with her, so they let us stay together. The only time she was out of our sight was when they took her away for tests. The news of Aria's accident spread through the high school and many of her friends began to gather in the waiting room. I refused to leave her side, so Jay and

Cody took turns keeping her friends posted while we all waited for test results, diagnoses, and instructions from the doctors.

Aria suffered four broken bones in her face. Her nose was broken in two places, the bone between the nose and mouth was broken, and there was another fracture in her face. She had lost her four front teeth and needed stitches on her lips. She had no other broken bones, but they told her she would be deeply bruised all over her body, especially the hip that had taken the initial impact from the van. The doctors believed that because Aria had stayed conscious after the accident and during the ride to the hospital, she hadn't suffered any significant brain damage. They told us they really couldn't determine if there would be residual damage for about a year, but felt optimistic because there was no real swelling or bleeding in her brain. Gratefully the tests showed she had no internal bleeding. They thought it would be safe to take Aria home, as long as we kept a vigilant eye on her. They also explained that because of the severe swelling on her face and in her mouth that her recovery process was going to be slow and painful. While we were waiting for the doctor to suture her lips, the nurse came in and said, "The gentleman who was at the scene would like to come in and see Aria." I had no idea who that could be, and I started to protest, but Aria seemed to really want to see this person. We had no idea what happened at the scene yet, and I had completely forgotten that it was a stranger who had left a message on my cell phone a few hours before.

I agreed that he could come into her room as long as I could stay too, so the nurse let him come in. He was visibly shaken and had tears running down his face. He walked in, grabbed Aria's toes and with relief said, "You look a lot better now, than you did a few hours ago." Aria smiled at him and said, "I know." I was confused until I realized that he was the person who had called me. I walked over and gave him a big hug, thanking him profusely. Before he left, he gave me his phone number and asked if I would update him in the next couple days so he could know how she was faring. George became a big part of our lives during the first year that Aria was recovering.

The staff kept Aria under observation for several more hours before they felt comfortable discharging her into our care. We were given several prescriptions and detailed instructions on what to watch out for in the next 24 hours. Aria's shirt had been cut off her when she arrived at the hospital, and her friends put together an outfit for her to wear home. It was a beautiful and sweet moment when Cody brought in the shirts, a sweatshirt, and shoes from her group of worried friends. The hospital gave us a plastic bag with her bloodied and cut apart clothes and shoes, and sent us on our way. That evening, I washed her clothes and put them back in the same hospital bag where they still sit in my closet, a reminder of how precious life is with my children, and how it can turn on a dime.

Before we took Aria home, the hospital set up appointments for her with a dentist and an oral surgeon. We also had appointments with her doctor, an ENT and a neurologist. The emergency room doctors were extremely helpful, and thought it would be better for Aria's psychological health if her care was handled on an outpatient basis instead of admitting her.

We were busy trying to absorb all the information, feeling thrilled and grateful to be taking her home. We didn't think to ask what they meant about psychological health. The hospital didn't give us any information on Posttraumatic Stress Disorder, which is common in accident victims. None of the doctors or dentists ever stopped to talk to us about the psychological impact the accident might have on Aria. All her care was geared towards how she felt physically.

We were totally unprepared for the psychological damage that manifested in her 16-year-old mind. The continual appointments and procedures, her physical injuries and the horror of thinking she was going to die when the van hit her, were having a tremendous effect on Aria's ability to cope. It wasn't until she had several appointments with her neurologist that she began to get the help she needed with the psychological effects of her accident.

Two days after the accident, one of the first police officers at the scene called and told us what had happened that morning. Aria truly was fortunate to have survived the accident. She was hit in the crosswalk by a van traveling 30 miles an hour on a four lane road. The van hit her hip; she bounced off the hood and fell face-first onto the pavement. The police told us she was lucky to be alive, and that they would thoroughly investigate every detail of what had happened.

George, the Good Samaritan who had come to see Aria in the emergency room, wrote everything down. He wanted us to have an accurate eye-witness account of what happened that day. She had been in the lane closest to the curb in the crosswalk when the van hit her. All the cars in the other three lanes had stopped for her as she crossed the street. George was in the farthest lane from her. As soon as she was hit, he immediately ran to her, calling 911. He told us that as they were taking her away in the ambulance, he didn't think she was going to make it. He said he came to the hospital to find out the fate of the brave little girl who had tried to stand up after being so brutally hit. He told us that he had held Aria, and they talked the entire time until the ambulance came.

The afternoon we brought Aria home, Jay went to the accident scene and found her teeth and blood on the ground at the spot she was hit. The police were still there, and told him that nothing had been disturbed or cleaned up because they were still investigating the scene.

Besides the four bones broken in her face, Aria's hip and knees were damaged, and she will most likely suffer painful arthritis symptoms as she ages. She has had to endure several painful surgical tooth implant procedures and may have more in the years to come. She sustained mild brain damage, but with the right medication and a good medical team she has learned to live a full life. Aria has almost no memory of her life before the age of 16. She describes her life before the accident as a puzzle with several missing pieces, so she can't capture the whole picture. She speaks of her life as "Before the accident, and after the accident."

We are grateful every day that Aria survived. Although her life inevitably has some challenges because of it, we know she will persevere with grace and insight, gifts that she has always possessed.

From my journal ~

For Aria: The secrets of a 1000 lifetimes lay within those deep dark eyes. When she sits upon the water, she shares her burden with the ancient ears of the sea. Breathing in she closes her eyes, feels the crest of a wave wash over her and is at peace.

The day Aria came home, I went downstairs to check on Cody to see how he was holding up. When I sat down next to him, Cody looked at me and said, "Things will never be the same again."

PART 4

From my journal ~ Spirit Mirror

It feels like I'm standing in front of a mirror as I write this. Not the kind of mirror that reflects your outside self, it is the kind of mirror that reflects your psyche. It's the kind of mirror that reflects how you think, emote, or not emote, and feel. It is the kind of mirror that reflects back the years of psychological and emotional damage. Standing in front of the mirror I see that things have largely remained unchanged. But in my defense this is the first time I had the courage to even approach it. If I would have tried to stand in front of this mirror before, I wouldn't have seen any reflection. But now I'm willing to look at the effects of the trauma and how it has damaged my mind, and spirit, and shattered my soul. I have the courage to view my reflection, and begin to name what I see. I choose to think of this as a spirit mirror and even though it is difficult to view my reflection, I'm glad that I am brave enough to stand in front of it and write about what I see as the past that bleeds into the present.

Chapter 30
I THINK I'M GOING CRAZY

For over a year I was consumed with taking care of Aria, but in the back of my mind I carried vestiges of what happened when I got the initial phone call about her accident. I couldn't shake the sound or feeling of breaking glass raining down inside my brain. And no matter what I tried to tell myself, I couldn't dismiss the vision of the girl sitting at the airport. I tried chalking it up to lack of sleep and coming to terms with the new normal in our house. Still, I knew deep down inside that something was seriously off.

I was experiencing changes that I couldn't account for and didn't understand. I kept having flashes of someone's past. I didn't think it was my past because I had worked so hard the last twenty-five years, at not having a past. I couldn't remember anything in a congruent way that had happened to me before the age of twenty. I had memories of times spent with friends in the last few years of being a teenager, but my past before then was as dark as any black hole in space. I unconsciously followed the rules that had become as natural to me as breathing. I knew not to remember, not to talk, and that I had to protect my family at all costs. I did these without thinking.

Eighteen months after Aria's accident we had a pretty good handle on what her long term issues might be. I could feel myself relax a little and I no longer felt the need to put all my focus on her. That seemed to be a cue for my mind and body to start reacting to the flashback I had in my office that day. I knew I had been having trouble concentrating since then, but when Aria's need for me slowed down, my own symptoms started demanding my attention.

I found that I couldn't concentrate for more than fifteen minutes at a time. I was anxious, moody, and depressed. I was beginning to think that something was seriously wrong with me, and knew it wasn't physical. It was as if my mind was slowly slipping away and I couldn't control my thoughts. I believed I was going crazy.

Trying hard to keep any remnants of my denial intact, I told myself I was just sick and exhausted. But, I was plagued by one physical symptom after another. I was diagnosed with the flu, sinus infections, colds, pneumonia, and unrelenting fibromyalgia. Yes, I was physically ill but I knew that something else had to be brewing. Whatever it was, it was manifesting very loudly as physical.

Six months after I first noticed my concentration and mood changes, I also realized that my thinking was off. It was as if I couldn't make any decisions. I became so impaired that simple tasks at work were becoming impossible for me. I was more skittish and hyper-vigilant than usual and began to mistrust everyone. My nightmares increased and became much more vivid. Everything about my thinking was off. I didn't know that I was having flashbacks almost continuously because nothing was a trigger, yet everything was a trigger.

One afternoon while I was at the doctor's office, something clicked inside me and I knew that I needed a different kind of help, and fast. I could feel the cracks in my mind deepening and my sense of reality faltering. It's hard to explain, but I had a deep knowing that my mental health was hanging by a very thin thread that was about to break.

I sat in my car after I left the doctor's office that day, feeling a desperate need for immediate help. Not knowing where to turn, I called the only psychologist I knew of at the time. Aria had seen a therapist for a short while after her accident. I still had her card in my purse, so I called her. Thankfully she answered, and after hearing that I thought I was going crazy, she made room in her schedule to see me first thing the next morning.

I was a mess when I arrived at her office. I was so hugely relieved to have someone to talk to that things started pouring out of me in a voice and in words that I didn't recognize. I heard myself sounding like a timid and frightened child, trying to tell everything at once, in a desperate last-ditch attempt to let someone know what had happened to her. I got tremendously anxious and then suffered the biggest panic attack of my life. It took a very long time for Diane to help me to settle down, and she set up two more appointments for me that same week. I drove home exhausted and confused, feeling worse than I had when I walked in. I didn't understand at the time, that I was starting to break all the "rules" of the mind control that had been programmed into me at a very early age.

I began having panic attacks several times a day. I couldn't find a comfortable or safe place to be. I was feeling hugely unstable as the directives to kill myself if I ever talked, began kicking in. The shattering glass that I had felt in my brain was the wall that I had built to protect me from my past.

I was breaking all the rules by seeing Diane and talking about things that had been taboo. I still didn't have any cognitive awareness this was happening. All I knew was that I was terrified. I felt suicidal and didn't know why. I was cutting myself to try to get snakes out of my body. I was constantly losing time and in crisis most of every day. I was still trying to go to work even through the craziness, but my performance was suffering terribly and my boss was losing patience.

I was afraid for myself and terrified for my family. When I was at home, I thought the safest place for me to be was locked in my room. I holed up in there, crying and trying to find ways to ignore the directives I kept hearing in my right ear, telling me to cut my arm, stomach, and neck. My ear burned with the threats that my handlers had promised would play out if I ever talked. At the same time I couldn't talk myself out of seeing Diane. I had a deep and uncontrollable need for therapy.

In the safety of my room, I wrote. I didn't realize how many hours I was pouring into writing or the depth of what I was getting down on paper, because I was dissociated from the pain in my mind. At night, with my energy spent, and feeling safe enough to come out of my room for a while, I could see that I'd written pages and pages, but I still didn't believe that what was on them had anything to do with me. As much as I tried to deny all those words, I was haunted by the feeling that I'd written them because they were true. That scared me even more. I felt that I had completely lost control over my mind. I was beginning to lose large blocks of time, and found it increasingly difficult to account for how I spent my days. I felt as if I was teetering on the edge of insanity.

My therapist Diane was doing the best she could to keep me safe as my memories spilled out and my instability kept growing. As soon as I remembered something, I would work hard and fast to forget it again. She tried to help me understand that I wasn't going crazy but that I had repressed memories that couldn't stay hidden any longer. That made no sense to me. I was dealing with how out-of-control I was feeling, and I didn't care what the reason was. I just wanted her to give me something to fix it.

I was living in continual crisis. My flashbacks were increasing and I had no way to calm myself. Diane was helping me through immediate crises and also trying to do therapy, but I had no tools or coping skills to manage all of this. Unable to regulate my emotions or find ways to distract myself, I was continually flooded with feelings and hopelessly overwhelmed.

Within two months of starting therapy, I was too ill to work and was placed on long-term disability. I was a mess. My family was a mess. Because I had been our rock and our financial stability, everyone was floundering. I couldn't be alone for any length of time before I would decompensate and I needed almost 24-hour care to make sure I didn't act out any suicidal ideations. Our whole family was adrift on a very stormy sea. This level of chaos lasted for nine long months, with me often thinking that it would be best for my family if I just died.

Gratefully, my defiant survival instincts kicked back in. An intense need to protect my family was still at my very core. I listened to my instinct to find myself another therapist. One of my friends was seeing a counselor at the time, and had asked her about referrals for me. I followed up with the names immediately, and in March of 2009 I walked into Kevin's office.

Diane had opened the gate to my healing path nine months earlier, but it was Kevin, my healer, my teacher, and the one I would call my Sherpa, who truly started me on my journey. Walking into his office that day I began six years of a difficult and treacherous trek up the highest of mountain peaks, but that was also the day I began to claim my life and start to live, not just survive.

Chapter 31
THE STEEP MOUNTAIN CLIMB

I was a psychological mess when I walked into Kevin's office, barely in my body and just trying to keep myself alive. It felt as if I was literally standing behind myself, as if I was witnessing somebody else's life from behind them. I was driven by an insatiable need to tell him everything that I had kept secret for thirty years. At the same time, I wanted him to stop the memories from coming. Because I had buried everything so deep and vowed never to talk, I kept being shocked by what I said to him out loud. My voice was sometimes unrecognizable to me. I would stop and ask, "Did I just say that?" It was a paradox. I couldn't believe that I was saying those words, but I also knew that what I was saying felt true.

I was terrified. Overwhelmed by emotions, I doubted that I could ever be "fixed." But no matter how hopeless I felt, I was even more desperate to survive. My goal was to live until the next minute, and then try another minute. I was living on adrenaline and pure survival instinct.

In the first two weeks of therapy Kevin was assessing me, but we were both deciding if we were a good fit. Behind the scenes he was putting together a team of collaborators to help him learn techniques for working with a trauma survivor. He needed to decide whether he could commit to seeing me through a long and painful healing process. I needed to decide if I could trust him enough to let him work with me. Talk therapy would have to wait. Our first order of business was to craft a solid plan to keep me safe. That was not going to be a quick or easy task.

Among other things, he diagnosed me with complex Posttraumatic Stress Disorder. Kevin gently told me that considering the severity of my symptoms, it would probably take years to work through my trauma. I was astounded. I had no idea what any of my diagnoses meant in detail, but I was sure nothing could be so difficult that it would take years to fix. I told him I was certain I would be better in a year. He didn't argue; he just nodded his head, knowing that was what I needed to tell myself.

Six years ago, I didn't have any idea what PTSD was. Now it's a common topic on the news as our military personnel come back from active duty. Back then, it wasn't talked about in the mainstream media. Besides, how could I have PTSD? I hadn't just come back from a war. I knew Aria had a slight case of it after her accident, but that was a direct result of the trauma of being hit by a car. I was sure that given some time, I would settle back down and Kevin would realize that I was just anxious and depressed. Before long, I would be back to my normal routine.

But almost as soon as I started therapy, repressed memories started erupting faster than I could deal with them. I was barely functioning at home and still couldn't be left alone for more than a few hours at a time. I was constantly being triggered and in crisis. I was resisting medication to help ease my anxiety and depression, and I was completely overwhelmed.

Day after day, I recounted acts of unimaginable abuse to Kevin. I often dissociated when I was recalling events. That kept a nice scrim between my memories and me, but by dissociating I was allowing myself to forget what we were talking about. But my mind wanted to heal, so each time I forgot, I would have to go through the process of remembering the incident again, and then again, until I could hold onto the details long enough to talk a little bit about the abuse. I was still using denial and repression to cope. Even on the days that it seemed I could begin to hold onto what we talked about during therapy, I would quickly stuff the memories away and forget them again. During those early years, we started a tremendous number of sessions by going back to try and remind me of what we had just talked about.

Not only was I dealing with the PTSD symptoms, depression and anxiety, but the directives that had been programmed into me were becoming relentless. My handlers had worked very hard to instill messages about how to hurt myself if I talked. Kevin's endless task was to keep reminding me that those instructions were nothing more than programming, and I didn't have to listen to them anymore. Every time I heard a directive telling me to cut myself, I practiced saying, "No, that's just programming and I'm not going to do it." It took years before I could trust myself to weed out what was programming, from what was my own desperate yearning to end my emotional and psychological pain. My therapist, my family, and I, all worked hard to end the cycle of crisis that had overtaken my life. I had a solid safety plan in place, was learning distress tolerance skills, and was getting ready to begin the arduous journey of processing my past.

We had a strict set of rules in place for me. Since I'm a rule follower by nature, I had no problem complying. We started with the basics. I committed to not hurt myself and allowed myself to talk about what had happened. I remembered to eat, to ask for support if I needed it, and most importantly, to ignore all the programming.

The first eighteen months of therapy I was still very much in survival mode. Kevin stayed fully present and supportive, and never made me feel that I should stop talking or recalling memories. We didn't necessarily address the memories I was having, since it was clear that I was nowhere near ready to begin processing them. He was working hard to develop a trusting and healing therapeutic relationship with me, but I went in and out of trusting him. I kept waiting for the day when he would leave me, but that day never came. Even when I tried as hard as I could to push him away, he patiently assured me and then reassured me, that he wasn't going anywhere.

We began using a metaphor for my healing process. We were climbing a mountain together. Kevin was a mountain climber himself and explained to me that when you start off on a trek, you don't look at the whole mountain. You focus on the next three feet in front of you. I immediately connected to this metaphor and began to see Kevin as my Sherpa. We both loved that image. A Sherpa's job is not to pull you up mountains, but to guide you. I began to look at my first two years of therapy as training for the climb. Once I had the safety skills I needed, we could begin the trek. One of the tasks Kevin set before me was to craft a personal legend, what I wanted as an ultimate goal. I thought about it and told him that my personal legend was to not just survive, but to *live*, with my eyes wide open, blinders off. So with Kevin as my Sherpa, we began the climb.

When we first started the memory-processing work, my emotions would sometimes get so intense that I felt as if I would die from them. I felt out of control and wanted to get out of my body. I wanted to scream or tear things apart, sometimes even wanted to tear myself apart. I would literally want to rip my skin off because I wanted to be anybody but who I was. I cried an ocean of tears in Kevin's office, more than once begging to be somebody else with somebody else's past, not mine.

I was experiencing derealization and depersonalization on a regular basis as the emotional pain stormed through me. Sometimes I felt like I was sitting in the room, but not really there. Other times I became so dissociated from my body that I would be surprised by the sight of my own hands. Sometimes I was sure Kevin was moving backwards. Sometimes the walls would seem mushy or the auras in the room were overwhelming. At those times, I couldn't keep myself grounded and my instinct to dissociate was overwhelming. I would do anything possible to block the intense emotional pain.

Kevin always stayed calm and would remind me to use my grounding tools when that happened. He would have me touch the wall until it felt hard again. He would ask me to describe the texture and the temperature of the wall on my hand, and remind me to stay present, remind me that I was okay.

I made a conscious decision to not research any details of my mental health diagnoses, or any memories that were resurfacing. I didn't want to put anything in my head that wasn't already in there. I wanted my memories to be my own, pure, without any information from other sources. I felt confident that what I was reporting to Kevin was the truth and not coming from something I'd exposed myself to and then repeated. The memories I was sharing were mine. They were nothing I had read, and were not shaped by any external suggestions.

Because I was constantly triggered and memories kept surfacing so quickly, Kevin imposed a "puppies and kittens rule." This covered what I could take in through the Internet, TV, movies and books. I could watch as many puppy and kitten videos as I could stand, but no violent shows or anything about mind control or programming. To this day, I still try to adhere to that puppy and kitten rule. Besides keeping my triggers at arm's length, it has helped keep my memories from being tainted. I will admit there are times when I need the validation that bad things happen to other people and not just me, and I'll seek out violent movies or TV shows. In a weird way, that helps calm me. I don't violate the rule very often, in fact, hardly at all. One of the main reasons I keep myself in check is that when I do break the rule, I feel compelled to report myself to Kevin and my family.

In July of 2010, I woke up from a dead sleep and felt a rush of emotion. Before I had a conscious thought about what I was doing, I grabbed a sharp object from my nightstand and began to scratch apart my right arm. I got out of bed and started punching the floor over and over again. My knuckles were bleeding profusely. Only a few minutes after I had opened my eyes, the blood from both my arm and my knuckles was dripping all over my bedroom floor.

When I had finally exhausted my energy and realized what I had done, I started wiping up the blood with a towel, but I didn't think to attend to my self-injuries. I didn't feel any pain. I was completely removed from myself. Jay got home as I was wiping up the blood and called Kevin. Aria also texted Kevin when she found out what I had done. Jay followed my therapist's instructions and immediately put me in the car. We set out on the long drive to another state and a program that specialized in treating survivors of severe trauma. Kevin had spent a few days shadowing the director of that program, and thought it would be a good fit for me.

He had called ahead and they were expecting us when we arrived. They offered both inpatient and outpatient programs. Typically, the outpatient program came on the heels of being discharged from the inpatient setting, but because they trusted Jay to care for me every night, they let me attend as an outpatient for a week.

I was hugely embarrassed, confused, and frustrated. I had let myself down in every possible way. Going into a hospital was everything I had tried to avoid. In my mind, I was a complete failure. I felt I had let everyone else down, too. I thought that Kevin would be so disappointed in me for going into crisis and for hurting myself that he would be too frustrated to continue working with me. None of this was true, but I couldn't see that in the shame spiral I was going down.

In the hospital I learned that what I woke up feeling that morning was rage. I had never experienced that emotion before, so it was foreign and overwhelming. Since then I have felt that same intense rage in my healing process, but now I know how to recognize, name, and ride it out without hurting myself. I learned that when I turned my rage inward, it took the rightful blame off the people who had hurt me. They deserved that rage, not me, nor my body.

My trip to the hospital was an intense and effective learning experience. The director of the trauma program took me under her wing and made room for me in her schedule. I stayed in contact with her for about a year after I was discharged. She helped me with feelings of confusion and anger countless times.

Even though I was only away from home for five days, I had a really tough time when I first got back from the hospital. The director helped me understand that what I was feeling was normal, and she helped me navigate talking to my children and a few close friends about where I had been and why.

Then I got sick. Even though I didn't realize it, I was run down and had no energy. I got the flu and one cold after another. Dissociating had actually been giving me a break from dealing with the trauma. Since I didn't have the need to do that as much anymore, I was getting run down trying to live with the truth while still learning coping tools.

Then I got the news that most people dread more than anything. I had two softball-sized tumors growing in my chest wall and I needed surgery. When the biopsy came back, the diagnosis was cancer. I had two surgeries within four months of each other. I have been cancer-free for almost five years now, and I fully expect that I won't have to deal with it again.

For most families, dealing with cancer is traumatic. My PTSD was so severe that cancer was more like an irritant, a blip on our radar. As a family, we often stop and remind ourselves that we live in unusual circumstances. We understood the seriousness of my cancer, and I'm grateful to be a survivor, but we're still forced to deal with my mental health symptoms every single day.

Kevin learned at a conference, that using a keyboard to journal could help with symptoms like mine. Keyboarding bilaterally stimulates the brain, and findings suggested that it made journaling more tolerable and it reduced the fear of being triggered. He thought this might be another possibility to help me face my memories, and move through the emotional and psychological impact of my trauma.

I was totally unprepared for the depth and ferocity of the emotions that my journaling brought up, and was soon faced with a whole new set of challenges. But by writing it all down, and facing the flashbacks, memories, and nightmares, a congruent timeline started to emerge from the dark. I was beginning to have a past.

It was still a constant struggle for me to hold onto the truth of that past. I would remember a piece of it, work through it, and then push it away. It was so hard to learn to trust the process, and to face the fear by holding the truth and sitting with it without dissociating.

I had recovered the memory of being told what was expected of me in the tunnel, but I told myself I couldn't share it with Kevin. After all, that was the day I was told I was going to die. But as much as I tried to withhold the truth of that day from him, I couldn't begin to let the past settle in and claim it, if I left out this critical piece of my story. That all changed in the summer of 2013.

I was having a terrible time making it through the 4th of July that year. I was constantly being triggered because my neighbors were lighting big firecrackers all day and every night. During our therapy, Kevin and I were processing my trip overseas. I was dropping hints all over the place about what happened to me in the tunnel, but I couldn't bring myself to say what I'd been told there. I was terrified of retribution and I was experiencing horrendous flashbacks.

Once that holiday weekend was over, Kevin told me he had figured out what I had been hinting at the past few weeks. When I confirmed his guess, something happened. Or, I should say, something *didn't* happen. Nothing happened! He was sitting across the room from me telling me what he thought my mission was, and no one burst into the room to hurt us. Incredibly, I began to believe that I might actually be safe. I knew it would be okay now, to talk with him about the details of my second trip to the Middle East. We had found the missing link. Finally, after processing what happened during that trip and my fears, I was able to hold onto the things that we talked about in a session. I began forgetting how to forget.

From my journal ~ My PTSD

It doesn't matter if it is cold, hot, sunny, snowing or raining.
There is no telling when it is going to strike.

Are they alive or dead?
Is that pain real or echoes from pain long ago that
Resurface with a memory?
It's like being held hostage by your mind
Thinking that today would be the day I am free.

I look like everyone else.
I know the difference between right and wrong.
Yet in my head I often can't remember
The last ten minutes of my life, or what day, year or time it is.

Are those smells real or is that a smell from a place and time
when I
Was being held against my will?
Am I really hearing the sounds of helicopters, planes,
Cicadas and birds?
Or is that the sound coming from a place that no longer exists
and
Should never be talked about?

I want so much to be like everyone else.
So I will keep pulling myself up the rope,
Out of the clutches of PTSD and all the skeleton hands of the
past that
Keep trying to pull me down.
I am like everyone else only my job is to live, so I CAN live.
That is all I can ask of myself if I am going to have a future.

Chapter 32
MY HEALING JOURNEY

My PTSD symptoms still have a solid chokehold on me. That is the best way to describe how it feels. I wake up every morning with the best of intentions. Even if I wake up from a violent nightmare, before I get out of bed I set the intention to surround myself and often someone I love, in peace, or I look out my window and declare that today is a new day. Almost immediately, I'm triggered. My therapist uses the phrase, "triggers, triggers, everywhere" and he's right.

My flashbacks can start within five minutes of my getting out of bed, especially if I take a shower (a trigger). I can hear the wind blow a certain way (a trigger). I can look out at a beautiful full moon (a trigger). I can be sitting in my living room and hear a car backfire, fireworks go off or someone coming up the stairs (all triggers). Given my past, triggers come from a huge number of places.

I also have flashbacks that are trauma-specific. In other words, when my mind is ready to deal with a particular trauma, my flashbacks around the event will increase. I have flashes of the incident until I spend time processing what happened, releasing both the memory and the emotions, as well as the feelings my body or psyche experienced during that time. When I've done the work around that abuse my flashbacks abate and give me some breathing room.

Another symptom that is hugely frustrating for me is my inability to concentrate. I was the major breadwinner in our family. I was proud of my career choices as well as my ability to grow and change with ever-expanding interests. I was easily able to concentrate and problem solve.

PTSD robbed me of my ability to concentrate. I am not able to complete more than a two-step task without getting overwhelmed, and I can't attend for more than two hours. Even if I take breaks and rest or walk around, I'm unable to get my brain engaged again to concentrate. It simply stops working. If I push myself, I get exhausted to the point that I'm open to negative thoughts and feelings, or unable to use the tools I need to stay grounded. This symptom chews away at my self-esteem more than I'd like to admit. I tell myself that therapy and getting better is my full-time job and most of the time that works; but when we are short of money I feel the frustration begin to creep in again.

Another symptom of my PTSD is my disordered eating. I have issues with certain colors and textures of food. I know where that came from, but I'm not able to work on and eliminate this particular symptom yet. Sometimes I crave a certain food but when I look at or try to eat it, my stomach churns and I feel ready to vomit. I have a "no vom" rule that I'm grateful for.

I also have major difficulties in the kitchen because of programming. I was programmed to cut my arms with a knife. My family got rid of all of our knives with white handles, but I can easily feel helpless or embarrassed about not being able to cut up food, or having someone come up behind me and say, "I'll do that," because they're afraid I might cut myself. These are some of the effects of my trauma that I'm not able to work on right now.

I used to love going to the library and spending time among the stacks and rows of books. I would choose one, sit down, peruse through it, and find another and then another, until hours flew by. I love being in the company of books. One of my PTSD symptoms is that I am no longer able to go to the library, grocery store, coffee shops, or crowded areas without support. The choices can overwhelm me and I stand there frozen, trying to fight off panic attacks. I also have trouble with choices in restaurants. If there are too many options on a menu, I get overwhelmed and struggle to make a decision. If I'm with someone I don't know well, I choose to eat whatever they order, whether I like it or not. If I am with someone I trust, I ask for help navigating the menu. We have done some "in-vivo" therapy, and will continue to do more.

I'm still plagued by nightmares and wake up screaming. During the work week my husband sleeps in a separate room so he can get some good rest. When we do sleep together, he's always ready to put his arm around me and tell me I'm okay if I wake up screaming.

I struggle with all these symptoms and a few more every day. It's been far from easy to go from the independent rock of our family, to feeling so debilitated by my symptoms. I'm dependant on family and friends. This is how debilitating, painful, and, hugely frustrating it is living with complex PTSD.

So how do I live with all these symptoms and not just give up and let them completely take over my life? I made a commitment to myself. I wanted to *live*, not just survive. I wanted to live in my truth with blinders off. I know with all my being that I cannot be the light I want to be in this world if I don't recover. I can't be a role model for my children and continue to grow, unless I recover from what happened to me and conquer my PTSD. It sometimes feels too big to conquer, but my personal legend is tremendously important to me. It motivates me during the most difficult moments of every day.

I'm still learning and accepting how much my past trauma impacted every aspect of my mind and body, spirit and soul. I have therapy three times a week, I read, I have a magnificently supportive family and circle of friends, and I continue to seek out and build a network of people who live, grow, and change with the seasons. I keep my eye on my goal.

In the fall of 2014, I had an amazing experience. I finished the first draft of the book you are reading. I have written the truth. I decided to publish this book for a few reasons. At first, I was just writing down my story to tell my Sherpa in a congruent way what had happened to me, and how I was feeling about it. Then I started to think that maybe others who were going through, or had been through trauma, might find something in these pages they could relate to. I also thought that this book could be helpful to someone who has a loved one with PTSD, to help them understand why that person acts or thinks the way they do, or to simply hear what it feels like to be a victim of trauma.

Even though my story is heartbreaking, I wanted to stress resilience, the ability to survive and eventually thrive. Six years into my journey, I have reached the summit of many mountains. I am optimistic about having a beautiful life. In fact I already have one. I am still very much in the middle of my healing journey. It's never been a linear process, but there is always growth.

In the early months of 2015, my daughter Aria, Kevin, and I presented at a conference in Florida. We presented as a panel, sharing our stories as a survivor, a caregiver, and a therapist in a five-year retrospective of my healing process. It was amazing for me to look into the eyes of other survivors and have them nod in affirmation, and then to answer their questions. My goal for being on that panel was to simply touch one person in the audience so they didn't feel so alone.

I trust my journey of growth and change is never-ending. I begin each and every day ready and willing to claim my life, my truth, and my health, and to stand tall with blinders off and my eyes wide open. The story of my life is my truth, and no one has the power to take that truth away from me ever again.

Acknowledgements

My beautiful family: Jay, more than yesterday, less than tomorrow. Cody, your shining essence makes our world a happier place. Aria, you embody grace and have infinite patience. Janet, I thank you for always being ready to harmonize with me. Patty, the Painted Journey continues. Suzanne, you are a beautiful wordsmith and my mirror. Sharon, I'm eternally grateful for our lifelong friendship and your support. Mary, Shari, & Scarlett, words can't express my gratitude. Simon, I out ran the tiger. Thank you for being my sentry by the meadow. Kevin, my ever patient Sherpa; you helped hold my fear as I struggled for my mind and my truth. You had my back for every arduous step up the mountain. I'm untangled and I thank you!

Made in the USA
Middletown, DE
10 August 2015